JOHN RUS

A
KNOCK
IN THE
ATTIC

TRUE GHOST
STORIES & OTHER
SPINE-CHILLING
PARANORMAL ADVENTURES

outskirts
press

A Knock in the Attic
True Ghost Stories & Other Spine-chilling Paranormal Adventures
All Rights Reserved.
Copyright © 2021 John Russell
v2.0

The opinions expressed in this manuscript are solely the opinions of the author and do not represent the opinions or thoughts of the publisher. The author has represented and warranted full ownership and/or legal right to publish all the materials in this book.

This book may not be reproduced, transmitted, or stored in whole or in part by any means, including graphic, electronic, or mechanical without the express written consent of the publisher except in the case of brief quotations embodied in critical articles and reviews.

Outskirts Press, Inc.
http://www.outskirtspress.com

ISBN: 978-1-9772-3937-2

Cover Photo © 2021 www.gettyimages.com. All rights reserved - used with permission.

Outskirts Press and the "OP" logo are trademarks belonging to Outskirts Press, Inc.

PRINTED IN THE UNITED STATES OF AMERICA

Disclaimer

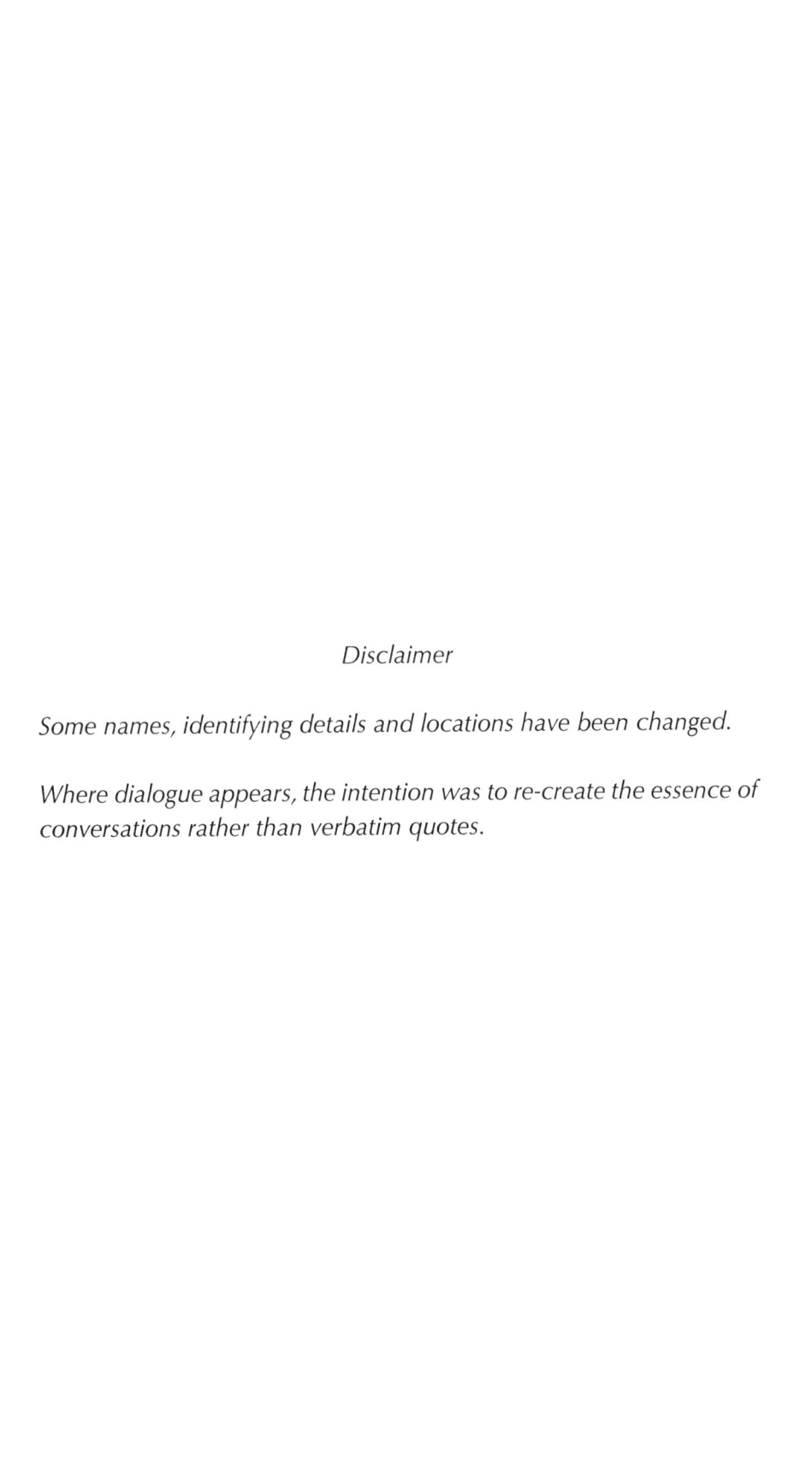

Some names, identifying details and locations have been changed.

Where dialogue appears, the intention was to re-create the essence of conversations rather than verbatim quotes.

Also by the author:

Riding with Ghosts, Angels, and the Spirits of the Dead
Publisher: Outskirts Press (September 8, 2020)
Available online wherever books are sold.

Table of Contents

Dedication i
Foreword iii

1. A Nocturnal Visit from an Old Black Ghost 1
2. Phantom's Footsteps... 4
3. A Russian Bomb?... 13
4. Strange Days, Indeed 18
5. Growing Up 25
6. Go Your Own Way.. 33
7. Paying My Dues 42
8. My Dad Died 47
9. Losing My Religion 51
10. Back to the Egg 55
11. A Belated Christmas Miracle.. 71
12. A Major Friend 85
13. New York, New York 94
14. On the Trail of the Assassin 103

15. Salem 108
16. Cornwall/The Haunted Camera.. 111
17. A Knock in the Attic.. 115
18. Uri Geller 119
19. Signs 125
20. A Very Unstable Stable 131
21. Florida 136
22. Keep a Good Sense of Humor.. 146
23. Farewell for Now 155

Dedication

I Dedicate A KNOCK IN THE ATTIC to:

The old black ghost. Thank you for opening up the portal that has allowed me to experience, so far, over 800 wonderful supernatural events in my life.

I would also like to acknowledge:

Spirit, for the inspiration; Marjorie, for her love; Eric, for being a son and a friend; and Melissa, for the freedom.

Special thanks to:

Bill Henderson, who, that night at Taste of Italy, encouraged me to write again.

Martha Lawrence for her friendship and mentorship over the years.

Carolyn Schurr Levin, Attorney at Law, for her legal guidance in vetting my book manuscript.

Jim Mullen for his insightful pre-editing skills.

Davina Zarnighian for being a great friend and beta reader who made excellent suggestions along the way.

Alexander Shagivaleyev for the many years of friendship and encouragement.

Rex Burke for the friendship across the years and miles, and the chess games.

To all of the radio and podcast hosts who have invited me to appear on their shows.

To my publisher, Outskirts Press; what a great publishing team to have behind me.

And I owe much gratitude to all of those both on this side and the Other Side who have helped to make my life the fascinating adventure it has been.

Foreword

JOHN RUSSELL IS an unusual man. He used to deliver office supplies for some years, and I got to know him when, on a delivery, he happened to notice a particular Van Gogh poster in my office. He said something piquant about it, we began to talk, and not long afterward I was looking at his portfolio of abstract expressionism and other assorted works. I asked him to do a painting for me, using the colors of Texas birds and wildflowers, which were somewhat softer than his own taste. He did. I now have a brilliant acrylic that I value to this day.

So I first knew Russell as an artist. I came to know him better as an insightful talker. For a number of years, he would just stop by and rescue me from computer screens giving headaches and keyboards promising carpal tunnel syndrome. For fifteen to thirty minutes we would talk about something, usually art, or politics, or philosophy. He knew quite a lot about many subjects. He argued well and for years my impression was that he was pretty much a thoroughgoing rationalist who liked to paint. I could live pretty easily with that.

Then later Russell loaned me a copy of Carl Sagan's last work on science and the paranormal. Which I read. It seemed pretty straightforward to me: there was no scientific basis for Para-normality, so one could infer that there was not anything to it, which is what I thought anyway. That Russell loaned me the book seemed to reconfirm his rationalism to me. But when I returned the book, I got a surprise: he asked me if I'd ever had a paranormal experience. Said he'd had many. Said most people he knew well had had at least one. My thoughts stopped short. But I was polite, jocular, and said I'd have to think back to remember. I did not know what to say and eventually changed the subject. But eventually the subject got changed back.

From that point on Russell began to tell me about his experiences. I remember his telling me about the gas leaks at his home, when they occurred. He did not put the emphasis on the paranormal when he discussed them at the time, except that he used the term "guardian angel," I thought, metaphorically, for his good luck. For that was a situation that could possibly be explained by simply, extraordinarily good luck. But there are other things that Russell says that defy explanation, at least any kind of explanation that makes sense to me, such that I am compelled intellectually to hold my tongue.

Russell knows this is the way I am. It does not seem to have discouraged him from telling me his experiences nor of telling others with his book. He knows I am profoundly skeptical of accounts like his, yet he did ask me to write this foreword. I do not know what to make of the apparitions he has seen, or the rocking chair that rocked on its own, or the curious sack of cans, or the object that floated across his yard, or his sighting of the UFO in downtown San Angelo, or…

What I have come to find by knowing Russell is that when it comes to a book like his, there are for the most part two kinds of readers. The first rejects the book out of hand; it makes no sense to them; it offers accounts of events that are so bizarre they dismiss it. The second believes it, swallows it whole and fits it into some kind of personal metaphysics, which to me is as bizarre, if not more so, than the very events Russell describes in his book.

I do neither. I accept the book as sincere, for John Russell is sincere, if he is anything. I wonder about the accounts in it; some are odd, some troubling, some amusing, and all mystifying in some way. Moreover, John has told me things about myself that he would have had no way of knowing, things about my family history that I'd even forgotten. I accept that without explanation as well. It makes more sense to me to do that than to invent a theory that makes no sense.

Thus, generally, I just listen to Russell. I enjoy his conversation; usually it is full of insight. And I enjoy his book. I hope you do the same.

—James Cogan, San Angelo, Texas.

CHAPTER 1

A Nocturnal Visit from an Old Black Ghost

NO NOISE WOKE me. I was just suddenly wide-awake for no apparent reason, and I was also without any post-sleep grogginess: My mind was as clear as a bell; my senses were on full alert. I didn't hear, or at first see, anything unusual. But then, as I rose up on my elbows in my bed so that I could look around, through my open bedroom doorway I saw an old black man's face peering around one of the doorways from down the hall. He was clearly visible in the night-light's glow as he gazed down the short hallway into my bedroom. He was looking right at me, staring me straight in my eyes. I was just five years old, and I screamed bloody murder at the top of my lungs, for my family was white and we didn't have anyone black living with us, so I fearfully assumed an intruder had entered our home.

To compound my fright the old black man responded to my scream of distress by venturing a few steps into the hallway. He stood facing me, and the glow from the night-light illuminated him clearly as he stood with his feet slightly apart and his arms hanging by his sides. He wore a red plaid shirt, khaki pants with a black belt, and black dress shoes. As I stared in disbelief he maintained his steady gaze, his eyes never once leaving mine. Feelings of terror overwhelmed me as my heart thumped in my chest, and my mouth was so bone dry I'm surprised I could still scream, but scream I did, a blood-curdling howl even louder than my first, and still the old black man stood staring at me.

1

He was not smiling. But neither was his look menacing. His close-cropped white hair gave him an almost regal appearance as he stared at me with a benign, slightly bemused expression as if he were intrigued by this strange white child who was howling like a banshee.

By now I was sitting straight up in bed, the tears streaming copiously down my face, and as I screamed again he began to disappear. Starting with his feet he began to vanish a bit at a time: his lower legs disappeared, and then his thighs, and then his arms and torso until all that was left of him was his handsome face, that face now floating in the air without a body to sustain it, and his face was still wearing that benign, slightly bemused expression until, at last, his face was gone, too.

As my parents came running I began screaming at the top of my lungs that there was someone in the house (even though I'd just seen him disappear), and I begged them to turn on the lights and look for the old black man, who I described to them in a sobbing voice. So powerful was the sense of reality and urgency I conveyed that while mom held my shaking body close and tried to comfort me my dad turned on every light in the house, and he looked through every room and even in every closet. I think I remember that he even looked under the beds. Dad checked all of our exterior doors, and of course, they were securely locked. None of our windows had been broken into. No one had come into our house. No one in a physical body, that is.

And after finding no intruder in our home and also discovering that our house was just as secure as when we had retired for the night my folks insisted it had all been a bad dream. A child's nightmare, perhaps provoked by watching something on TV that had unsettled me and had made its way into my subconscious and expressed itself as a night terror of some sort.

I knew better.

I had seen someone. Someone who was just as solid as you or me, someone who had subsequently vanished into thin air when I saw him and began to scream. And with a shiver I finally realized what else I had just seen: I had seen my first ghost.

Even though my parents attempted to comfort me and left the hall light on for me it took me long hours to get back to sleep. I peered down the hallway wondering if the ghost would come back, and what he would want with me if he did. Why was he visiting me in the first place, scaring me to death in the middle of the night? How was it possible that he could appear in a body with clothes that were every bit as solid as yours or mine, and then vanish like a mist? And why did he vanish when my parents came running in response to my screams? If he came back again, what would he say to me, what would he ask me if he were to talk to me? Would he want me to do something that I would consider scary? Would he hurt me? There was a whirling dervish of questions in my frightened mind, but there were no answers.

From sheer exhaustion I finally dropped back off to sleep.

I never saw the old black ghost again, but I remember him as clearly as if the incident had happened this morning.

He was only the first of many ghosts I would come to see, the harbinger of the beginning of my psychic, mediumistic, paranormal life, a life lived at the edge of the Veil which separates the seen and unseen worlds. He opened up the way. He opened up the door.

So, to that old black man, that old black ghost: I never knew your name, Sir, nor have I seen you since; but it is to you that I fondly dedicate this book. Because you opened up that doorway and allowed me to see, I've had over 800 incredible paranormal experiences in my lifetime. I've been able to show others the way, and to help many people because of the ghostly contacts I've been afforded. I've been startled; entertained; puzzled; and, because of those normally invisible folks on the Other Side, I've had my life saved several times.

Thank you, Sir, for opening the portal. It's been one incredible journey for me, and as for you my friend, I hope you found your way. And if you can, please come to see me again. It's hard to explain, but I've kinda missed you over the years. And this time, I promise not to scream.

CHAPTER 2

Phantom's Footsteps

I ENDURED MUCH distress and many tribulations as a result of the old black ghost's visit: it was hard, as a five-year-old boy, to accept parental reassurances at bedtime and to enter into my haunted bedroom with all of my senses on edge, feeling all of the strange unseen energies swirling around me, and wondering if this would be the night when the ghost would return and scare the bejesus out of me once again.

My days were spent in fearful wonder with frequent glances over my shoulder just in case there was something haunting me and gaining on me.

My nights were spent expending large amounts of energy in trying to relax and ignore the rising tide of feelings and sensations that were threatening to engulf me.

For lack of a better explanation there were unseen energies that I could feel around me. I didn't know who, or what, these energies were. They didn't communicate with me; they just aroused these emotions in me which I couldn't begin to define or explain or understand, but I somehow knew that my life, at the tender age of five, had dramatically changed and had somehow been irrevocably altered forever, and I didn't know why.

And no one around me, not family or friends or neighbors, could adequately explain to me what had happened to me and why. At the young age of five years old I had begun to feel isolated and alone, a feeling that would haunt me to some degree or another all the rest of my life.

Now, if the ghost had visited me and had then left me alone, and nothing else spooky had ever happened to me, the ghostly visit in and of itself would have been a life-changing event, as well as something that I would have remembered to my dying day, and I would have talked about it to others provided the circumstances were right. But life would have—eventually, I presume—returned to some semblance of "normal."

But such was not to be my fate.

It seemed that the old black ghost's purpose in visiting me was to open a portal of some kind, a doorway into the supernatural realm where those on the Other Side could come through and visit me. And visit me they did.

My dreams became uncannily vivid, and sometimes they were prophetic: I would see something happen in a dream, and then days, weeks, or months later I would see it happen or become aware that it had happened in the "real" world.

Strange people who I did not know came to me in my dreams, calling me by name, speaking strange things to me that I could not always make sense of or understand.

And then, "It" happened: The defining moment in my life when I was aware that I had somehow crossed the boundaries that separate "normal" perception and "extranormal" perception. I was playing in our back yard when a car pulled into our driveway and a man and a woman got out. I went inside to alert my parents, and they came out to greet these friends of theirs with whom I was not acquainted. While they were standing outside together greeting each other and making small talk, I had a vision about my parents' friends. Exhibiting the tactlessness of childhood I interrupted their conversation thusly:

"You folks just took a vacation. You stayed at a big hotel with two or three stories to it that was painted this [certain] color on the outside, and it had trees that looked like this [I provided a description] growing in front of it that you could see when you pulled up, and in back was a big blue swimming pool with white chairs all around it."

Their eyes bugged out as they looked at me. They were speechless and stood as still as stone. The silence from the adults was deafening in its roar. I had, come to find out, accurately described their vacation, the correct color of the multi-story hotel that they had stayed in, the trees that were growing in front of it, the pool area, and all. I pointed to their car in the driveway.

"And you went there in that car. But you took kids with you. You don't have kids with you now, today, but you took kids with you then. And you also—"

"John." My father's voice. "Hush." Emphatic. I got quiet.

"I'm sorry," my mother began, "but you know kids. They have quite an imagination."

Their friends still hadn't moved or spoken; they just stood there a moment longer, staring at me as if I had cobras growing out of my forehead.

"How the hell could he possibly know all that?" the woman asked.

My mother and father exchanged confused glances.

"You see," the woman continued, "we have just returned from our vacation. That's what we were coming to tell you all about, because we had such a wonderful time. And we took the kids with us, in our car." She nodded toward the driveway. "That car. And we stayed at a hotel with several stories that was painted the exact color John said, and there were trees out front that matched the exact description John gave. The pool area was exactly like he described it." She looked at my parents. "You didn't even know that we were going on vacation, much less where we were going or where we were going to stay." She looked at me again, and I'll never forget the mixture of fear, curiosity, and amazement in her eyes. "How the hell could he have known all that?"

I'll never forget the wide-eyed look of fear and amazement with which she gazed at me.

"John," my mother's voice this time, "go play."

"Yes ma'am. It was nice to meet you folks."

And off I went clutching whatever toy I had been playing with, and from that day forward I could tell people about their past, their present, and their future, as well as intimate details about their daily lives and thought processes, even to the emotions they were feeling and why.

And sometimes, I could tell their exact thoughts, word for word.

I guess I came to be a pretty spooky little bastard to be around by all normal counts: I don't remember those folks coming to visit with my parents ever again.

Then the footsteps started.

We had a large yard and my parents had taken great pride in hand pouring concrete curbing which outlined and defined flower beds. While the concrete was still wet my mother inlaid stones, inscribed sayings such as "Faith, Hope, Charity," and had us press our hands into the wet concrete so as to leave a record of our handprints. My parents also poured concrete sidewalks throughout the yard, and some of those sidewalks wrapped around several different corners of the house, many times only a few feet away from the house itself.

Mom frequently wore high heels, and dad often wore dress boots with roping heels; you could hear either of them coming from a mile away, click-clack-clicking or clomp-clomp-clomping as their footsteps echoed off of those hard concrete sidewalks.

I don't know what it is about being a little kid that makes it especially fun to hide and then jump out at the last moment and scare someone, but I got both mom and dad more than a few times by hiding just around the corner of the house and then jumping out as I heard their footsteps come to within a few feet of where I was hidden. As long as they stayed on the sidewalks it was impossible for them to fool me: I always knew where they were at, and if I wanted to I could also run around the outside of the house playing hide-and-seek and they could never catch me.

So I was in the side yard one day when I heard the screen door open and close, followed by the staccato clicks of mom's shoes on the sidewalk in the back yard; she was heading in my direction.

Suppressing a giggle, I walked to within a few feet of the corner of the house, crouched down, and grinned as I calculated how close mom was by the increasing volume of her footfalls. When her steps were so loud that I knew she would be turning the corner of the house within a few seconds I jumped out and yelled "Boo."

Imagine my surprise when the sound of the footsteps immediately ceased.

Imagine my amazement at the eerie sound of silence that hung over the yard.

Imagine my shock at discovering that not only wasn't my mom, nor anyone else, on the sidewalk, but that the entire back yard was as empty as a broken heart.

I remember standing there with my mouth hanging open, staring at the empty space where my mom should have been. Now my eyes were bugged out. I looked around the yard, and then I took tentative steps along that very same sidewalk where I had so clearly heard loud footsteps only moments earlier. I walked along the sidewalk until I came to the back door. I turned away and walked around the corner of the house farthest from where I had hidden. I then turned around and retraced my steps. I simply couldn't believe that I had heard loud footsteps so clearly and that no one was there.

I finally just stood still and listened for a long time; nothing.

I shrugged and went back to my play. As I rounded the corner of the house to the side yard where I had originally been the footsteps began again, as clear, and as sharp and as loud as before, once again coming in my direction.

This time I decided to run around the corner of the house, determined to catch the prankster before they could disappear.

I only had a few swift steps to go before I rounded the corner of the house, and the footsteps on the sidewalk were just as close and just as loud as they had been previously.

I rounded the corner of the house expecting to collide with

whoever was there, but as I slowed to a stop once again the sound of the phantom's footsteps fell eerily silent and just as before there was not a soul in sight.

It had to be my mom. She had to be playing some kind of trick on me, and I raced to the back screen door, flung it open and allowed it to slam shut behind me as I raced into the living room. There mom sat in her chair, reading, or watching TV or whatever, a startled look on her face.

I think I blurted out something on the order of: "I caught you." But I think that I knew in my heart of hearts that my mom had not been responsible for the phantom's footsteps. She was a grossly overweight woman, and although she could move pretty swiftly for one so large I was young and lithe and swift of foot and on her absolute best day there would be no way that she could outrun me. Besides which she was wearing house shoes, not hard-soled dress shoes.

Several generations of my family had been both believers in and had had experiences with the paranormal. We all seemed to attract our fair share of strange experiences; however it would turn out that I would be destined to attract not only the largest number of experiences, but the most dramatic ones as well.

Anyway, that day of the phantom's footsteps produced one of the first of many long talks with my mother, all with serious overtones, about the unseen realm of life, spirits, ghosts, hauntings, strange experiences, and more.

It was a lot for a young boy's mind to absorb and try to understand, but one thing my mother told me stuck with me, took root, and eventually bore fruit: and that was that I didn't have to fear any of these experiences, because they were not going to harm me. These ghosts, spirits, whoever or whatever they were, were intent only in getting my attention and letting me know that they were there.

Perhaps they would want me to try to convey messages to others for them. Perhaps they had things to tell me about myself that would prove beneficial to my own life. Perhaps they were just lonely, and wanted to talk, wanted to communicate, wanted to interact with someone whom they found to be interesting as a person for whatever reason.

And the old saw is true: Children are especially receptive and open to supernatural experiences. As children we haven't yet erected the walls and barriers—emotional, psychic, and otherwise—that keep us from experiencing the Other Side. It's only as we grow into adulthood and are subjected to ridicule, shame, taunting, and embarrassment that we begin to push away those on the Other Side and we also begin the process of shutting down any awareness whatsoever of that realm of life. For example: "Stop lying, Timmy, you do not have an 'invisible friend.'" "Judy, you have not talked to your dead grandfather. Such things are impossible, and they just don't happen. We all miss him, but you're going to have to stop making things up." "Richard, don't lie to me. We all know there are no such things as ghosts, so a ghost couldn't have taken my earrings. Now, what did you do with them? Tell me, and I won't punish you, this time."

It's a shame that so many people lose this wonderful and perfectly natural gift. And for some it's awfully hard to open those doors again once they've closed them so firmly for so many years.

I, however, was lucky: I had the good fortune to grow up in a family where my psychic gifts and talents and paranormal experiences were not made fun of but were actually encouraged. So I came to my mother more and more frequently with my experiences, and she did her best to explain them to me and to encourage me to continue to develop my gifts.

And it wasn't just me having these experiences. My mother and I began to share in many of these experiences as I magnetized an increasing number of spooky occurrences to me, and my father even became a reluctant participant. As did our quite unwilling cats and dog.

My father was, I think, actually a "closet believer" in the supernatural. But he had seen that a belief in the unseen realm had made other people look foolish. He had no doubt observed that a belief in psychics and psychic phenomena could bring down the wrath of the Church. But I believe that his biggest reason for trying to ignore all the supernatural goings-on was that the experiences scared him. The experiences were beyond the pale in more ways than one, chief of which for him was that they were something that he couldn't get his hands on and confront at will. He was brave enough to combat a man physically when he had to, but he couldn't effectively strike a ghost. He was at the mercy of something, someone, who was invisible and who couldn't be touched or grabbed and yet that something or someone could manipulate physical reality.

These experiences manifested to him when and where and how they wanted, and he not only had no control over that, but he couldn't provoke a physical confrontation either. In the "real" world, he was a physically strong man capable of handling himself in a barroom brawl as well as working his ranch all day. In dealing with this invisible realm he was entirely out of his element and without know-how.

So it would cause my dad much consternation when we would all be together in the yard (all within sight of each other as we would only be standing fifteen or twenty feet apart) and all of us would simultaneously hear the mysterious footsteps on the concrete sidewalks. I remember once my dad dropped his gardening tool and barked out his version of the word hello: "Hal-lo?" This was in response to some particularly loud and particularly close footsteps we had all just heard, and by God my father was going to find out once and for all just who the hell was making these strange noises around our house.

He set off around the house in search of this mysterious trespasser and my mother and I exchanged glances and began to laugh, for we knew that he would not find anyone in the flesh. Sure enough, he walked around the house, searched inside the house, and, of course, found no one in a physical body. He returned to where we were, picked up his gardening tool and tried to recommence work as if nothing out of the ordinary had happened, but we weren't going to let him off the hook that easily.

However when we tried to discuss it with him he merely hooted "Aw" and moved off to another section of the yard where he couldn't hear us giggling and also to where I'm sure that he hoped that he would not hear the phantom footsteps again.

But the footsteps stayed with us, following us around the yard for many years.

Eventually my father showed less of an inclination to perform yard work. By way of explanation to us he attributed his lack of enthusiasm to advancing age, but I'm fairly sure the sound of the footsteps he experienced over the years had a lot to do with him abandoning his customary outdoor chores.

Our pets also heard the mysterious footsteps. In response to the sounds of the footfalls our cats would sometimes run away as if their tails were on fire, and Midge, our little mongrel dog, would sometimes raise her hackles, growl, and make a beeline for the back door, where she would whine to be let inside and then she would subsequently refuse to come back out into the yard.

The noisy footsteps outside continued to happen throughout all of the years that we lived there, but their outdoor frequency and intensity lessened in later years; the footsteps migrated indoors, and they were just as loud and just as frequent as they had been in the yard, causing our friends who came to visit no end of consternation. But that's a story I'll reserve for tales about the haunted dinner parties we held in later years.

CHAPTER **3**

A Russian Bomb?

AS IF I were some kind of psychic lightning rod which attracted the increasingly bizarre, paranormal phenomena began to escalate, seemingly centering itself around me as if I were the focus of attention for these strange manifestations; and of course the mysterious, unexplainable, and downright spooky also continued to occur in our home and in our yard.

But we also saw a couple of things that, while certainly mysterious and more than a little creepy, might have been easily explainable by whatever our military was capable of at that time. Like the little metallic looking "blimp" that flew through our yard one sunny Saturday morning.

I was about six or seven years old I guess, no more than eight or ten, and my father and mother and I went out in our back yard fairly early in the morning (before 9 a.m., I recall) to do some yard work. Well...they were doing yard work; I was there to play. I remember it was a bright, sunny day with not a cloud in the sky. I was relishing the beauty of it all and enjoying the fact that my parents were outside with me, performing their customary duties of maintaining our yard. It was pleasant to have their company while I played.

I was playing with a length of rope; I hadn't yet decided if I was going to be a cowboy or Tarzan swinging on a vine. Mom and dad were working close to the alley, while I played on and around a big old mesquite tree that sat right about in the center of the back yard. So I saw it before they did, it being out of their line of sight.

There it was, floating silently about 10-15 feet above the ground; it was about two feet long, shaped like a blimp, metallic looking, and it had a small rectangular-shaped antenna which was slightly curved, made of open mesh, and it rotated atop a small shaft a few inches in height which protruded from the top of the blimp-shaped object up toward the blimp's nose area.

When I first saw it, it was moving through the neighbor's back yard, the neighbors that were directly across the street to our south. It was moving very slowly. Absolutely silently. No smoke, no noise, no flames. Just the slow, gentle forward movement and the steady spinning of the little rectangular antennae as the craft navigated its way through the tall brush and trees of our neighbor's yard and started across the street. Toward our back yard; toward us; toward me.

"Mom. Dad. Come look. Quick."

Something in the tone of my voice made them drop their tools and come running. When they looked to where I pointed, my father's face became anxious, and my mother grabbed his arm. "Oh my God," my mother exclaimed as she searched my father's face for reassurance. "Honey, what in the world is it?"

My father was tense and silent, and all of us watched as the little blimp slowly made its way across the street, and then it entered the perimeter of our yard.

Now, I've got old pictures of our yard and our neighborhood as it was back then, and the neighborhood was very lush: Yards were filled with big trees, shrubs, and bushes both tall and short, scattered flowers and flowerbeds, tall sunflowers, and roses on trellises; not to mention all the sheds and garages. Suffice it to say that the fact that this little blimp successfully navigated this veritable jungle without so much as grazing a tree limb is a feat of enormous proportions in and of itself.

By this time, my parents were beginning to slowly move to one side of the little blimp's flight path as it flew slowly through our yard, its little antennae spinning away (Think of the Munchkins parting for Glenda as she floated down as a large sphere of light and you get the picture.). Again, there was no hum, no noise, no smoke, and no fire or flame—just this slowly moving silent phantom of some kind. And my reaction? Well, I knew I had the opportunity of a lifetime staring me in the face.

Ignoring Midge, our little dog who was furiously barking her head off, I ran for my rope. This was much too good a prize to let it get away. Indeed, God must have known how much I would love such a toy and sent this delight my way. I thought of how my friends would envy me as I showed off this marvelous phenomenon to them. I'd be the star of "show and tell."

As I quickly fastened a lasso and I began to whirl the loop around my head in preparation for flinging my rope skyward to capture this precious object my father yelled but two words, but he yelled them with such force and with such urgency that I immediately let the rope fall limp to my side: "John. No."

I reluctantly shifted my gaze to my father's worried face.

"My God, John, it may be a Russian bomb. It could blow up and kill us all."

Now you have to remember, those were the days of high Cold War tensions, and to my paranoid father if the facial tissues didn't come out of their box correctly it was a Russian plot of some kind.

So I, thoroughly dejected, had no choice but to watch as my prized treasure escaped ever so slowly through the air into the neighbor's back yard, and then just as slowly on through successive back yards, causing numerous yelps, yells, and cries of shock, fear, and astonishment as it flew by and was sighted by neighbors performing their weekend yard chores.

I begged my parents to let me get on my bike and follow it, or to let me run after it on foot. As slowly as it moved I could have easily kept up with it by just walking very slowly underneath it as it glided silently along.

My begging and pleading fell on deaf ears as my parents gathered at their fence with neighbors who were now congregating to make sure others had seen what they just saw, and that they weren't all indeed going crazy.

We watched the little craft fly out of sight and listened to the yells and whoops of neighbors as they spotted the little craft for the first time, and I remember my parents debating whether or not to call the police. I can't remember if they did. I was too busy watching my prize fly away, never to return. What wonderful pleasure such a toy could have brought me.

Slowly, the neighbors drifted back to their yards and their yard work and I, enthralled and speculating wildly, gathered up my rope and tried to resume play, all the while keeping an earnest watch toward the skies and neighboring yards, just in case it should come back, or in case there were more like it coming our way.

I never saw it again.

I had many questions concerning the incident we'd all just witnessed, questions my parents couldn't answer, and I wanted to know why they couldn't.

"John, there are some things we just don't know."

I could never shake the feeling that if they had let me follow the little craft, I might have gotten some answers.

I don't know if the little blimp was a military device, a bizarre weather balloon of some kind, or something either from space or the paranormal realm, but that wasn't to be the only sighting of a strange object in the skies at our home.

One of my mom and dad's friends had come to our house for a Sunday afternoon visit. After her visit, as she was leaving, we all stepped out into our front yard to walk her to her car, and we all spotted a strange object hovering in the sky. It was solid black, shaped like a box kite, and occasionally it released a small amount of wispy black smoke from its bottom. My mom, my dad, our friend, and I all saw it, as did a few of our neighbors, and I also recall a couple in a car stopping on the side street, rolling down their car window and asking what we were looking at. We pointed and told them, and they drove up the street to the east to get a better look for themselves.

I ran inside and got my little telescope, came out and set it up on its tripod, and through its lens I could see the object better. It was just a black rectangular shape, four-sided, that looked like a big black metal box kite. That was it. It had no markings or features of any kind, and it hovered there for the longest time before finally, slowly, moving off in a southerly direction. Other than the occasional wisp of black smoke, there was no flame, no other motion or manifestation of any kind, and no sound that we could hear.

Again I will concede that these objects could very easily be explained as the product of some military's technical capabilities, but they're still remarkably interesting when you spot them. They cause quite an uproar among the witnesses who see them.

But the following occurrences I will now relate to you can't be explained by anything military. Unless the military was specializing in ghoulies and ghosties and other things that go bump in the night...

CHAPTER 4

Strange Days, Indeed

MANY OF MY friends ask me how it felt to grow up in such an environment, having had such frequent odd experiences.

It's like anything else: what's strange at first becomes familiar through repetition. And in my case familiarity would breed a comfortable association with the many phenomena I've experienced over my lifetime.

From the ages of about five to twelve years old I didn't see too many more ghosts in solid form, certainly nothing as dramatic as my sighting of the old black gentleman; although I did hear, and see, other phenomena: Doors in our old house would open and close by themselves. Usually I only heard them open and close, as I would most often be in another room. But I remember more than once I did see a door swing shut all by itself. There was no one in a physical body near it, and no breezes or drafts of any kind in the house. As a matter of fact, many of these experiences occurred during the winter months when the house was closed up tight with all of the windows and doors snugly closed and locked so that there was no possibility of any of these manifestations being caused by winds or drafts.

One such door-related phenomenon I remember very well, as it was close to Christmas when this particular incident occurred, and what's more memorable in the timeline of a child's life than Christmastime?

My mother would sometimes go next door to visit our neighbor; she and my mother had become close friends, and often my mother would leave me in our home by myself, during the afternoon for example, while she went next door and visited for an hour or so. I was never afraid of being by myself. I knew how to use the phone to call for help, and I had the neighbor's phone number handy in case something happened so that I could call my mom, and I knew how to call the police. And as a matter of fact I came to relish and enjoy those times when I was alone. It made me feel very grown up and in charge.

And my mom made sure that all of our windows and doors were locked up tight, so I never felt afraid. I knew I could get to the phone quickly if something happened, and mom would only be a minute away.

So on this one particular afternoon she had gone next door to visit and I was "flying" one of my spacemen through the house. I had started his journey in the living room, pausing to look longingly at the pile of beautifully wrapped gifts under our Christmas tree. I then flew him back through the dining room, the kitchen, into the breakfast room, and I was heading for my father's bedroom when I heard his closet door swing shut on its noisy hinges and close, the wooden door making solid and audible contact with the wooden door jamb, followed by the latch audibly clicking shut. I had even seen doors open or close by themselves and usually either mom or dad or both would be home with me, which lessened to a degree the spooky feelings that I naturally experienced when witnessing such a sight. Sometimes the door events didn't bother me at all, but there was something weird about my dad's closet: I didn't know it at the time, but I came to realize in later years that this particular spot in the house seemed to be the strongest one of many portals into the unseen dimension of life through which spirit activity could pass back and forth and manifest itself on the physical realm in such a way that we could perceive it.

For some particular reason that to this day I'm not sure I can identify, the sound of that door closing, and latching caused me to creep out way beyond reason.

I didn't call my mom. I didn't suspect that an intruder was in the house and call the police. Instead I knew what to do, and how to do it.

I ran as fast as anyone has ever run in their life and I zipped next door, where I pounded on the door so loudly that I nearly caused both my mom and her friend to have a heart attack, and when my mom, who was closest to the door, opened it, I was breathing so hard I could barely talk.

My mother and her friend were both terrified, thinking something horrible had happened, a fire perhaps, or a break-in, or that I had somehow hurt myself in a terrible accident.

After I caught my breath I explained what had happened, and my mother's friend was so concerned she asked if we shouldn't call the police.

Mom was sometimes pretty intrepid, so she assured our neighbor that we should be okay checking our house out by ourselves, but if we didn't call her within a specified amount of time she should then call the police and recount the incident to them so that they'd come to our rescue.

Mom and I went back to our house where the front door was still standing wide open just like I had left it in my haste when I had fled. It was a chilly day and a good deal of our home's heat had escaped into the outdoors by then.

Well, mom and I went through every single inch of that house, looking under beds and in closets, looking everywhere, and there was not a soul in sight, and not a thing even disturbed, much less missing or stolen.

She called our neighbor to report that everything was okay, and then mom told me very matter-of-factly that I had probably heard one of our ghosts; that was all. My mom knew that I had already had many such experiences, as we all did in our old home, and she was curious as to why this particular incident spooked me so much. I didn't have a satisfactory answer for either her or myself, but I was by now sufficiently calm so as to encourage my mother to return to our neighbor's house and continue her visit, which she did.

I knew the house was absolutely secure, absolutely empty of strangers, and I felt quite comfortable with my mother returning to the neighbor's house.

I was not scared to be in our home by myself, for I knew that there was no one there in the flesh, and whoever might be there in spirit surely would not harm me.

Mom returned to her visit. (Our neighbor was probably rather amazed, but she was familiar with the spiritual realm as well.) I returned to my play.

As I once again flew my spaceman through the house, I gathered up my courage and I deliberately retraced the same route as before in order to show both myself, and those on the Other Side, that I was not afraid, and, as I walked into the breakfast room, which was next to my father's bedroom, I heard the exact same distinct sound of the closet door closing and latching itself again. My hide crawled and the hairs on my body raised up.

I knew no one physical was in the house so I boldly marched into the bedroom, walked to the closet door, and yanked it open.

Of course I saw no one, but the strangest chill came over me, a chill that wasn't caused by our home's loss of heat, for it had already warmed back up to a toasty coziness. The closet itself, and only the closet, was actually cold, almost ice cold, as if I had walked into a meat locker. The rest of the room was comfortably warm.

I closed the door, made sure the latch was engaged, and resumed my play. I was now just a little cautious about that room; not fearful, just cautious.

I distinctly heard the door close one more time that day, after I had already shut it and checked to make sure it was secure.

The "dropped marble noise" was one of the strangest things of all, and something none of us ever figured out. We couldn't relate it to anything "normal," such as normal house, plumbing, or furniture noises, nor could we relate the noise to any relatives who were deceased and might be trying to communicate with us in such a strange fashion. It didn't seem to be an attempt by anyone on the Other Side to communicate anything.

Here's what would happen: In the middle of the night, usually a little after midnight, there would be a sound like someone had dropped a big "shooter" marble from ceiling height onto our wooden floors. The "marble" would hit loudly, bounce a few times, and then there would be a sound as if it were rolling clear across the floor.

The noise was so loud it would wake up the entire household. It usually occurred at least two or three times in a single night, the intervals from occurrence to occurrence varying each time. After awhile we quit investigating it, and just listened to it, unable to fathom its meaning (if it even had any). So on some nights one or the other of us would hear it and the others had become so accustomed to the noise that they would keep on sleeping soundly. It's amazing what you can accustom yourself to when the paranormal is normal.

But it was rather bizarre to hear that loud, sharp sound of something hitting the hardwood floor, bouncing, striking a few more times, and then rolling across the width of the room. Especially when the sound repeated itself several times in the same night.

We never felt afraid, though; simply curious.

And, oddly enough, we never discovered what it was, or what its meaning might be.

Like the footsteps, we frequently heard the dropped marble noise for a lengthy period, and then it finally—abruptly—quit happening. We reached a point in time when we never heard the dropped marble noise again. But the sounds of footsteps continued, now moving inside the house as well.

There were also very loud and prolonged creaks in our cane-bottomed chairs, the type of sounds that they made only when someone actually sat down in one of them.

This was another source of amusement for my mother and me, and a great source of consternation for my father.

Everyone knows that houses, both old and new, settle, creak, groan, pop, and snap.

And that a cat or a squirrel running across the roof can sound like a herd of elephants. Furniture, especially old furniture, makes more than its share of strange noises, especially during weather changes as its wood expands and contracts due to environmental changes in the atmosphere.

But if you pay life any attention at all you soon learn to distinguish between such noises as natural plumbing, house, furniture, or animal noises and those noises which are caused by someone or something.

There's a distinct difference in the sound made by wood expanding or contracting and subsequently popping or groaning due to weather changes than there is when someone substantial sits in a chair, for example.

We had several of these cane-bottomed chairs scattered throughout the house, and we had some outside, too.

If you've ever sat in an old cane-bottomed chair you know the distinct sound it makes as the cane produces prolonged groans and creaks and pops. The sound is quite unlike anything else on the planet, and the only way to replicate that sound it is to sit down in a cane bottom chair. No other sound approximates it.

Well, these cane-bottomed chairs would let out that very loud and prolonged creak and groan, with all the subsequent ticks, squeaks and pops that they continue to make as a person sits there and they settle in and the chair adjusts to the pressure of their weight; but our chairs would make these noises when there was no one visible sitting in them.

The chairs were so loud, so noisy, and so obvious, that on one occasion my father, who was coming into the kitchen for some additional breakfast refreshment, stopped and just stared at one of the chairs, which continued to pop and creak loudly as if someone were shifting their weight back and forth. Dad looked at my mother, and then he looked back at the chair, and then back at my mother with a quizzical look as if to say, "How the hell can this possibly be happening?"

My mother would always use such an occasion to further her spiritual proselytizing, explaining to dad that we had an unseen visitor in the house who was making him or herself comfortable in the chair.

Most of the time dad would just snort and go on about his business, but on that particular morning I remember him standing there dumbfounded for a long time, for he had grown up with cane bottom chairs, and he was intimately familiar with their sounds, their creaks, and their adaptations to weather changes.

He also knew what it sounded like when a person sat in one of those chairs.

He finally gave my mother one last look, shook his head, poured himself some more coffee and headed back to finish his newspaper in bed.

And it wasn't just the cane-bottomed chairs that exhibited the evidence of a ghostly sitter.

Occasionally one of the rocking chairs would move by itself, making slight, small rocking motions for a good minute or so.

Again, this would occur on days when the house was closed up and there was no possibility of a breeze or a draft, and all pets were accounted for.

CHAPTER 5

Growing Up

FOR ME GROWING up was a constant nightmare: I wanted the pleasures of a stable, happy home life, and the material security I saw my peers enjoy; and instead, my parents fought viciously and we constantly experienced financial woe and serious lack of everyday material security; mom and dad knew how to portray themselves as being successful, but we were always in serious debt and we lived, for the most part, on borrowed money.

I aspired to health and athleticism, and instead I was scrawny and constantly sick; I craved social acceptance and popularity, and instead I was an outcast.

And the more I tried to fit in and the harder I tried to figure things out, it seems the worse things got.

I was bullied and tormented at school, and then I was bullied and tormented at home. I had a half-sister ten years older who had already left home, so I didn't have an ally in my house. My overprotective mother rarely granted me the privilege of playing with any of the neighbors' kids and therefore I normally felt the pangs of isolation and solitude. So I devised a physical escape: I would play outside for hours and hours, or I would ride my bike up and down the street and around and around the same block for hours at a time, and I also devised a nonphysical escape: I would escape into books, daydreams, TV, and I would draw.

I tried to stay below the radar so that my increasingly unpredictable and ever wrathful mother would be hard pressed to find a reason to lay into me.

The result of this imposed isolation seems strange in retrospect, but it was quite normal at the time: I became closer to the invisible side of life than I did to my physical family and my peers.

Growing up. Good god a'mighty, it's one of the toughest jobs we're given to do, isn't it? And it can be incredibly painful emotionally. Especially when you're way different: gay; colored; handicapped; foreign…psychic.

Kids are cruel; adults are crueler.

Kids taunt you with the little knowledge that has been passed down to them; adults taunt you with the little knowledge that they've chosen not to outgrow.

When you're young and you try to share a paranormal experience it hurts when you're elbowed in the ribs to shut you up; when you're older and you try to share a paranormal experience the metaphorical elbow to your ribs comes in the form of denigration. Or, as one of my best friends on this planet once told me: "Russell, people can make you; they can also break you. People can ruin you, destroy you." And nothing breaks a person any quicker than casting doubt on that person's integrity. Just ask the presidential candidates.

So as I moved from the realm of youth into the realm of young adulthood I thought I would have an easier go of things: I thought people would be more understanding, more accepting, and that they would act more civilly toward me. Lord, was I ever wrong. As I read somewhere recently, someone said that the adult world is just high school all grown up: you face the same bullies, the same prejudices, and even the same cliques, only now they're disguised. But if you dig deep enough you'll discover that all the grief from your childhood is still there, smoldering in the pit that you thought that you had buried it in, and occasionally that grief somehow gets fanned into flames once again.

It seems that jerks never change.

———∞———

As I grew into my teenage years the paranormal activity stepped up its intensity. I continued to have visual and auditory experiences, as well as olfactory ones. In specific places in our house we would occasionally smell the perfume of my deceased grandmother, for example.

This experience would occur after she had been dead for many years and would be localized in only one spot in the house. There would be a "zone" in which the fragrance would become apparent, but you couldn't smell it anywhere else. It would be a powerful, overwhelming aroma, and then it would suddenly fade and be gone.

And of course I continued to see startling phenomena.

People have naturally been curious about my family's religious beliefs, because—as you probably know—the Christian Bible casts aspersions on any paranormal manifestations except for its own…the ones that it sanctions.

Well…we weren't Satanists; nor were we Buddhists; nor were we adherents to any of the other countless belief systems out there. We were Presbyterians, members of a well-known and highly respected Presbyterian church in town.

We were in church nearly every Sunday; we attended Sunday school—kid's Bible study classes for me, adult Bible study classes for my parents—followed by all of us attending Sunday morning worship services. I know I was baptized, and I want to say it was in that Presbyterian church, but I really don't recall.

We practiced religion in our home, praying before our meals and at random times during the day. We studied the Bible. We had the almost obligatory pictures of Jesus scattered around the house. We wore crosses. We sang hymns, loved Gospel music, and celebrated Christmas in a serious and Christian way. And we also, unhindered by any contradictory biblical and religious power, held séances and continued to witness escalating paranormal phenomena.

Mom even taught adult Sunday school classes at the church for quite some time. It was there in that church, while teaching a class one Sunday morning, that she said she slowly closed the Bible and asked the class, "Is any of this working for anybody? Is this true and relevant for our day and time? The moral lessons are great, yes, and are appropriate for any day and age, but how many of us really believe in or have experienced these miracles spoken of so frequently in the Bible, and how does this relate to the many studies of ESP and other phenomena that we're beginning to become aware of? Can we just talk about what we need to experience in our daily lives, and not limit our knowledge to the Bible, or this church, or to some creed?"

She related to me that people turned their heads to look at each other, their body language, and facial expressions indicative of discomfort.

A brief silence reigned as nobody wanted to be the first to speak.

But finally someone had the courage to speak out, and when they did it slowly opened up the floodgates. It turns out that everyone in that Sunday School class was having similar thoughts to my mother's.

This posed a dilemma. No one wanted to abandon the Bible. No one wanted to run afoul of the church and its teachings. And no one wanted to go behind the minister's back. So my mother made the decision that she, and a few others from the class, would approach the minister and explain their thought processes to him, and if he put the kibosh on things that would be the end of it, and they would have no more such discussion during Sunday school classes.

They met with the minister, he listened carefully, and he agreed that there were many other spiritual areas worthy of study, and as long as they didn't abandon the Bible or get too far out in what they were teaching and learning in Sunday school, that they were free to openly discuss these other thought processes.

Everyone in the class agreed that none of these other belief systems were always workable either, but things were happening out there, and nothing was happening in the church, and weren't those things, if they proved to be beneficial, worth a look-see? Worth a thorough examination? Especially as there were some reputedly good benefits occurring from some of these spiritual explorations such as healings, etc.

And what about those who still believed that such goings-on were the work of "the devil?" Well, everyone agreed that the biblical injunction made sense, that if "the devil" was going about doing good then he was surely bringing down his own kingdom. (And he [Jesus] called them to him and said to them in parables, "How can Satan cast out Satan? If a kingdom is divided against itself, that kingdom cannot stand. And if a house is divided against itself, that house will not be able to stand. And if Satan has risen up against himself and is divided, he cannot stand, but is coming to an end.")

And then my mother upped the ante: for those who were more deeply curious and willing to be a little more experimental she would open up our home to a small group who would begin to meet weekly for a "prayer circle," "prayer group," or whatever you wanted to call it.

I think that it's important to note that in the group that began to meet in our home were those who devoutly identified themselves as "born again;" most claimed to be Christians; most were well-versed in the Bible; and there were even some of the Pentecostal and Charismatic persuasions. And most times the group opened with prayer in Jesus' name, recited the "Lord's Prayer," and so forth.

These people were seeking a spiritual manifestation that they were not experiencing in any of their churches: a genuine healing; an accurate prophecy; an angelic visitation. Some proof, some evidence, that God or angels existed, or deceased loved ones lived on. Some sign, some guidance, some daily help that was real and genuine.

They wanted to experience now, today, what had been written in books hundreds of years ago. They wanted the printed word on the page to come alive and to demonstrate to them that it was still meaningful, still powerful, still workable.

And most discovered that, after prolonged and serious study, the Bible didn't live up to its claims. One such example of many: "I promise that when any two of you on earth agree about something you are praying for, my Father in heaven will do it for you" (Matthew 18:19).

It was ridiculously easy to demonstrate that Jesus' promise didn't hold water: there were many sick and dying who had not just two praying for their healing, but a multitude praying in agreement for their healing. Most didn't get well, and many died. Those that did get well got better as a matter of natural fact, their bodies gradually healing over the course of time. There were no miraculous healings.

I can't think of many things that are more heartbreaking than a great many people gathered together in prayer, people who are fervent in their faith and belief, mightily invoking Jesus and the Heavenly Father in Jesus' name and everyone praying in agreement that the five-year-old child suffering a brain tumor will be healed, and then watching that child die.

Too many such heartbreaks occur repeatedly on this old planet every day, and yet we still desperately cling to that useless biblical promise and resort to reminding God—in vain—that his son gave us his word that if two, just two, of his followers here on earth would agree about something in prayer that God Almighty would do it for them.

Well, I (and others) had seen that promise fail so many times that we knew that we could not put stock in it.

And so this was the motivation behind many of our prayer group's members: our religion doesn't work; is there something that does?

Well yes...there were (and are) some things that do work. The only problem is they work so sporadically, and the mechanisms of their working is so unfathomable, that the quest becomes ever more frustrating.

It almost feels like the universe rolls the dice and interprets the result by consulting some Cosmic Dungeons and Dragons game: you get healed; you don't. You win the lottery jackpot. You don't.

But some of the results that began to be in evidence from the prayer group's meetings were remarkable.

Now you have to remember that the church members were open to and actively seeking just such manifestations in the church, but the church's and the Bible's methodologies had sold them short.

In the prayer group meetings in our home people opened up to a variety of techniques and tried a variety of methods in order to better connect with the Other Side and to receive manifestations of spiritual power. Some techniques worked better than others. Some were ludicrous and were quickly abandoned. None were one hundred percent effective, but they were experiencing results, whereas in the church, confined by dogma, they had experienced nothing at all.

One area of major concern was health and healing.

Incorporating traditional prayer with various techniques from mysticism yielded spotty results, but enough people reported healings—or at least improved health—that the prayer group was encouraged to continue experimenting in that direction.

And then someone suggested that the prayer group pick out a subject who was known to them, someone who had been medically diagnosed with significant health problems, and the group would then "go to work" on that person, using prayer and a variety of techniques to seek to heal them; but…they would not let the person know of their experiment.

After several weeks someone would then phone the person and bring the conversation around to, "How ya feelin'?" And many times the person would either report a remission, a cure, or at least a vast improvement.

These were encouraging times for the group, and many began to have the feeling that, "The sky's the limit." If only they could find that magic key that would open the door to consistency.

It's hard to keep such a group cohesive and properly focused: a gathering like that is always subject to egos striving for recognition and dominance. It's hard for a person to forego their addiction to their own vanity. Instead of striving to maintain focus on the purpose and direction of the work certain people instead tried to turn the focus onto themselves, attempting to force their unwanted (and imaginary) leadership onto the others in the group.

Also, as in all things, the winds of paranormal change frequently blew, and first one person in the group and then another would bring in some "miraculous" new teaching, concept, technique, etc., that they would insist that the group should immediately adopt and practice.

There were some workable techniques in some of these philosophies, and some were sheer idiocy and folly.

And for some bizarre reason the weirder and sillier the philosophy or technique was the more determined the person would be to push it onto the group.

Such actions began to impede the group's progress. Tempers flared. Feelings were hurt. People became unwilling to overlook differences of opinion. Sides were drawn, and the group began to fracture, and then to splinter.

After several years of incredibly effective results vanity and egos got in the way to the point that the group all but ceased to exist, and splinter groups formed in other's homes...usually those with large egos who were seeking to build their own little following who would kowtow to them and tell them how gifted and wonderful they were.

It was sad to observe.

"Too many cooks..."

CHAPTER 6

Go Your Own Way

AS A YOUNG man I sat in on some of the prayer group meetings. It was there that I became aware of an interesting phenomenon: When I began to sit in on the meetings with some regularity, pretty, hot-looking women with great bodies and great legs would come to the circles dressed ever more scantily. Their makeup became more pronounced. Their skirts and dresses got shorter and shorter. Their hose or stockings got markedly sexier. And their heels got higher.

I didn't object, mind you. What red-blooded young man would? But what was interesting was that it wasn't only young and/or single women who exhibited such behavior, but older, married women who began to sex themselves up when they knew I would be in attendance.

And if you think the leg crossing and uncrossing scenes in such movies as Basic Instinct are exaggerated…well, they're not.

Things got so blatant, so brazen, that my mother actually spoke to some of the women about their manner of dress and their deportment and asked me to stop attending the group for awhile. Damn.

By that time I was a teenager and frustrated with the status quo anyway; I was frustrated with my life; I was searching for an identity; I was trying to make sense of my psychic gift while also wrestling with my typical teenage angst and hormones on overdrive.

It's probably good that I stopped going to the group…I'm sure some kind of interesting sexual tryst was imminent if I had stayed. Hmmm…maybe it's not so good a thing that I stopped going…

33

I don't want to dwell on my preteen years; nor do I want to dwell much on my teenage years. It was a time fraught with difficulties, including troubles at home with my increasingly abusive and insane-acting mother while not experiencing any help from my drunken father. We owned a bar, and my dad (again, actually my stepdad) would leave after breakfast and go open up his bar around eight or nine in the morning, and we wouldn't see him again until around midnight or later, with him having drunk nearly a case of beer every day.

This left me as the sole target of my mother's frustrations and wrath, and it's like she went out of her way to invent new and ingenious tortures with which to make my life a miserable, living hell.

I'm also reasonably sure that she had been poisoning me and other family members. There's strong anecdotal evidence to support that theory.

The trouble was I had Stockholm syndrome; my mother had so effectively crippled me emotionally, spiritually, and psychologically that I was incapable of becoming independent and standing on my own. I tried and failed; repeatedly.

I was also bullied at school—castigated by my mother if I fought back, and berated by her if I didn't. I felt like my life was a real-life version of *The Twilight Zone*.

I was denied the opportunity to make friends and to go to other kid's houses.

Punishment was not forthcoming for something I considered an egregious error, but she would erupt like a hateful volcano over something insignificant. And then reverse the scenario next time. Over and over.

For my entire life with my parents I felt like I didn't know if I was coming, going, or had done been. I was seldom ever praised.

If I accomplished anything noteworthy the response was, "Well, of course," said dismissively.

I tried to make friends, and I didn't really know how. I tried to date and to have a girlfriend, and I didn't really know how.

I tried to fix my messed up homelife and I certainly didn't have a clue as to how that could be done.

I longed, longed, for the lives that other kids had, when I caught brief glimpses of the manners in which they lived. And I was so damaged I couldn't for the life of me figure out how to begin to achieve such a thing for myself.

As I said, I'm not going to go into details here, but in later years I shared some of the more horrific things that my parents said and did to me with a close friend of mine. He stared at me for a long while, and then he softly said, "If I had grown up like you just described, I would have set my hair on fire, grabbed a machine gun, and gone on a murderous spree of destruction."

I shrugged and said, "I thank God that I didn't."

I did, however, run afoul of the law. It was like I was pushing the universe, pushing God, pushing my parents, even pushing my friends to see if anyone gave a damn; to see if anyone would stand up and say, "Enough. Enough of this path of self-destruction you're on. You're mending your ways now, and here's how to do it. Here's the path to take."

But no one did.

I stumbled around like a blind man in the dark, trying to find the way: Was I an outlaw? A criminal? A scholar? A wannabe athlete? An artist? A poet? A writer? Was I stupid, useless scum? Was I a genius? What in the hell, who in the hell…was I? I tried on identity after identity and in my heart of hearts I knew none of them fit; none of them were me.

But I didn't know how to find me.

If I hadn't been so damaged by my parents I might have been able to listen more closely to the Other Side and the guidance they were trying so desperately to give to me, but my brain and my life and my emotions were a whirlwind, and the voices seldom got through to me. But the Other Side did watch over me, they did keep me, they did help me, they did protect and save me…but the journey was long, and the climb was steep and fraught with danger, frustration, and heartache.

But…thank you, God. Thank you, Guardian Angels. Thank you everyone on the Other Side who has looked after me, watched over me, protected me, and comforted me…and not given up on me. I made it. With your help and guidance…I made it. Thank you.

I did have some very dear friends who took a shine to me for whatever reasons. They were few…but they were mighty. And much beloved. I didn't know how to be a good friend back to them. I tried my best, but I just didn't have the knowledge as to how to do it. I tried to reciprocate the best that I could. I know I fell far short, and it's a testament to my friends that they stayed with me, supported me, reproved me, and encouraged me.

Oh god how I wanted to tell them about my home life, about what I was enduring, about how desperately I needed to escape, to explain to them that I didn't know how to cope, I didn't know how to find myself, I didn't know how…to be me.

But in large part what kept me from trying to communicate these things to them was my pride. I viewed confession as weakness, and for most of my life I had also been rebuffed anytime I attempted to explain my situation to people, so…

(I was even made fun of for telling the truth. In grade school we were asked to explain what our parents did for a living. When my turn came I said that my dad owned a bar. Most of the class started laughing and the teacher got stern with me and told me to quit kidding around and tell the truth. "But I am. My dad owns a bar." The look she gave me conveyed her opinion of me, my dad, and his bar, and I endured lots of razzing from the other kids.)

But God bless my friends…they stuck with me anyway, through thick and thin.

And then in the midst of all of this confusion my real spiritual journey began in earnest.

My mother made a friend (I'll call her Rebecca), and this woman proved to be my salvation. I met her in the waning days of the prayer group in our home, and it was she who introduced me to the Ouija Board in a serious way. I had dabbled with a board before but she was a serious practitioner, and she showed me how to use the board as a serious tool and to obtain useful information. She also introduced me to crystal ball gazing, and many other occult practices.

She seemed to be amazed at my psychic gift, was highly encouraging of my development, and I was fascinated with her: She had lived a varied and interesting life, and I was enthralled with some of the tales she told.

She lived with a gentleman who was somewhat skeptical of the whole psychic and paranormal thing, but he was polite about his skepticism and somewhat open-minded.

She began to invite me into their home, and it became an eye-opening haven for me.

I say eye-opening for it was in their home, and under their watchful eyes and their kind judgment that I slowly began to understand that I was not the total loss that my mother treated me as being.

You have to understand something about my mother: she was a phenomenal con artist and a master manipulator. She projected such an effective façade that if you asked anyone who knew her they would tell you what a kind, loving, good-hearted and sweet person she was.

The reality was that she was one of the most hateful and venomous people I've ever known and a masterful liar.

So my mother would weave woeful tale after woeful tale to explain to outsiders how mistreated she was, when the reality was that she was the one who was always on a vendetta against the other family members, my father and myself included.

So Rebecca and her friend would compliment me, would talk to me about my good qualities. And it was through them that I began to get an idea of who I might really be: a person who saw things correctly, had some praiseworthy gifts and talents, and was of at least reasonable intelligence, with a great sense of humor and above average creativity.

Awesome. Now, what to do with it? I had no clue what I wanted to be when I grew up, much less how to get there.

While visiting Rebecca's house I had the opportunity to hone my skills as a psychic, providing readings for many of her friends. But my proudest moments were those when I provided a reading for the boyfriend with which she lived, and on a separate occasion provided a reading for the man's son and made both of them into believers.

Rebecca told me she had known many psychics, including some famous ones, but that she was more interested in me and my developing gifts than she had been in any of the others.

She was a source of comfort and support to me until her dying days, and I still miss her and think about her. She showed me the path and helped me to begin to navigate it.

Remember the neighbor with whom my mother used to visit while she left me alone in our house, the neighbor I spoke of back in Chapter Four when I had the bizarre experience with my father's closet door?

I had moved back home briefly when I was in my late teens after having lived in my own apartment for awhile. Our neighbor's husband had developed dementia, and it was a sad and astonishing thing for me to behold, for the man had been possessed of a keen intellect, was a fearsome chess player, built things such as an outdoor swing that their grandchild and I played on when we were just kids, handled all of his own yard work, and more. It saddened me greatly to see him mentally deteriorate.

And with his dementia he became violent: many times he would swing his cane at his wife. He also hallucinated, seeing people, critters, and objects that weren't there, and he would swing at them with his cane as well. Oddly enough I was the only person who could calm him down and handle him. He always responded well to me and would let me calm him, and I would sit and talk with him for awhile.

I was also the only person that he would allow to shave him. He'd sit for me, and I'd use his electric razor and shave his face for him. In spite of his dementia he still knew enough to stick his tongue firmly into his cheek to puff it out and give me a better and smoother surface on which to run the razor.

Now I had been a sickly child my entire life, and some of my health issues were serious and chronic. In spite of that I would push my body as hard as I could, when I could. I lifted weights; I practiced various martial arts. (Eventually, as I aged, I ran distance, covering five to ten miles during each daily run; I played tennis at a good enough level to defeat one of the players on our local university's tennis team; I swam up to a quarter mile at a time; I took up bicycle racing and would ride up to 300 miles per week at a brisk training pace; I hiked; I hunted; I fished; and more.) I kept myself as fit as my then current physical condition would allow, and I was always extraordinarily strong for my size, flexible, and I had good balance.

So our neighbor would call on me not only to help with her husband, but to perform some minor household chore or another from time to time, which I was always glad to do.

One such chore she asked me to do one bright, sunny day was to replace a curtain rod in their living room and rehang the curtains. In order to do so I had to climb up onto the top step of a small stepladder, which was three or four rungs tall.

The woman's husband was off in the den on the other side of the house, and she left me to my chore and went to supervise him.

I had almost completed the chore when, uncharacteristically, I lost my balance and began to fall, falling backward and to my left. Now...I was not alarmed. My body was fit enough (in spite of my health problems) and my sense of balance was such that I instantly determined a completely workable plan: I would allow myself to continue to fall but I would violently twist my upper torso as I did so that I would be facing the floor and I could land on my feet and hands, avoiding injury.

From my tumbling skills acquired from having studied Judo, and my whirling and spinning abilities (many times airborne) acquired from studying Karate, Kung Fu, Tae Kwon Do, and other martial arts I knew that I would be able to perform this maneuver and save myself.

But I didn't have to.

Before I could even begin to initiate the maneuver, and while my head was still basically turned toward the windows and the curtains, I felt a large, strong, and powerful hand at the level of my hip and lower back on my left hand side. (My first thought was that the man must have silently entered the living room and that it was his hand I felt so strongly on my body; the hand was much too large to have been the woman's, as she was diminutive in size.)

The hand not only stopped my fall, it gently but steadily and forcefully pushed me back to an upright and stable position on the ladder, holding me steady until I had completely regained my balance. I was relieved in spite of knowing that I could have saved myself from injury, and I breathed out a sigh, said "Thank you," and turned my head to see who had rescued me and nearly fell off the ladder again when there was not a soul in sight...at least, not in a physical body.

I knew what I was thinking was an impossibility, but nonetheless I immediately snuck quickly through their house and sure enough, they were both sitting in the den, the man watching TV and the woman knitting or reading or something. Like I said, I knew it would be impossible for one or the other of them to have so silently entered the living room, pushed me back onto the ladder, and then in less than one second's time to have left the living room, because I had turned my head immediately to see who had rescued me and no one was there. But I was so astonished that I had to reassure myself.

I snuck quietly back through the house to the living room, climbed atop the stepladder again, and put the finishing touches on my chore.

From time to time I couldn't help but turn my head to glance around the rooms of their home just to see if the ghost that had saved me from the fall would appear, but whoever it was did not make an appearance.

I finished my chore, stepped down and off the ladder, repeated quietly aloud a thank you, and went to inform my neighbors that the chore was complete.

It would not be the last time that invisible forces would continue to rescue me, saving my life many times in the years to come.

CHAPTER 7

Paying My Dues

ONE OF THE hardest things I ever experienced as a young man, and one that I still have no definitive answer for to this day, was one of the most hurtful, painful, and disturbing experiences of my life.

I mentioned earlier that I have a great sense of humor. That's one of the things that my friends have always loved about me. What they didn't know was that the humor was a coping mechanism to help me to deal with the pains and deep frustrations I experienced in life, mostly due to my unhappy and unstable home life.

Along with that sense of humor I was a little cavalier about things. Hell, I was young, had my whole life ahead of me, was still stupid enough to be deluded by an unrealistic optimism, and had yet to taste Life snatching away my most cherished things...and my most loved people. I could still genuinely comfort people over their losses without it affecting me too deeply emotionally. That backfired: I became the go-to person for anyone suffering any kind of emotional grief. But...I was able to endure it. Until one day an experience knocked me for a loop and opened up my eyes to a greater and more harsh reality.

I had already developed, in my mid-teen and late teen years, a reputation as a seer and as someone who could give comforting words of knowledge and wisdom to others. People would drive a couple of hours just to get an in-person reading with me.

So one day my mother asked me if I would go and visit a family consisting of a single mother and her two teenaged daughters. I knew, vaguely, about the family and their circumstances; I was not completely unaware because their names, and the family's circumstances, were broadcast all over town by nearly every religious and spiritual group there was. The circumstance was this: one of the daughters had a virulent brain tumor. She had already been treated at MD Anderson in Houston, but without success. And she was getting worse.

Now, by constantly having my finger on the pulse of the religious and paranormal community I was aware of what was being said about this girl, and it was melodramatic. Many of the churches in town, from staid mainliners to evangelical Charismatics and Pentecostals, decreed that God himself was going to dramatically heal this girl so miraculously and completely that it would spark a fire of revival in town that would spread throughout Texas and possibly even sweep throughout the United States.

Interestingly enough, the same sentiment was echoed, albeit in slightly different terms sometimes, by paranormal and occult groups in town. Everyone was in agreement that some higher power of some sort was going to heal this girl. There were no dissenting voices. Everyone had received, believed, and acted upon, through their particular set of religious beliefs, the vision, the revelation, that some higher power was going to perform a miracle for this poor sick girl.

I had never before become aware of so many different religious and spiritual belief systems having come together in one accord, one voice, one vision, and one testimony.

So that was the backdrop against which I made my visit one sunny afternoon.

The mother opened the door to my knock, and her face was worn by the emotional pain and worry she had carried for her daughter. The house was dark inside, even though the sun shone brightly. The brain tumor made the girl sensitive to light, so heavy drapes and curtains blocked out as much exterior light as possible.

The mother asked me to come in, and the gloom, both physical and emotional, settled over me like a wet heavy blanket. She led me to a room where the girl and her sister sat, and the second I laid eyes on the girl I heard a male voice, aloud, in my head. The voice clearly and distinctly said, without emotion, "She is mine. She will be with me within two week's time."

I was so astonished by the voice's proclamation that I didn't know what to do, what to say, or how to act.

I prayed fervently with the girl for her healing and tried my best to give her some words of comfort while her mother began to race through the house packing. The girl's head hurt so badly, and she was so ill that even as I sat there attempting to bring some prayer and hope and guidance to the girl, they were all already in motion to head out the door as soon as I left—back to MD Anderson where they hoped against desperate hope that maybe this time a cure would take, that maybe something would help.

The girl's mother walked me to the door, and I'll never forget the look of desperation in her eyes as she looked at me and said, "People say that you hear the voice of God. That you predict things, that you have insights, that you know things. Did God tell you anything today? Did God say anything to you that can give us hope?"

How in the hell could I repeat to her what the voice had said to me?

I muttered some platitudes about God being all-knowing and that he has a reason for everything he does and that we have to trust in his wisdom and other such idiotic nonsense.

I had been about as helpful to the woman as if I had thrown live rattlesnakes into her home when she opened the door to me.

Obviously disappointed and in horrific emotional pain, she nodded slightly and cast her eyes to the floor as she closed the door. I stood there a moment in the beauty of the bright sunny day, thinking what a contrast it was to what lay just on the other side of that closed door.

How many such bright and sunny days do we enjoy, driving blithely unaware past homes that may contain their very own private hell inside?

I walked slowly down the sidewalk back to my car, got in, sat there a moment, said an additional useless prayer, and then slowly drove away.

And within two week's time...the girl was dead.

There's a useless promise in the Bible, and this story illustrates very well the fact that the promise is a lie. The promise is this: "I promise that when any two of you on earth agree about something you are praying for, my Father in heaven will do it for you." (Jesus Christ speaking in Matthew 18:19)

Christ amighty; there were countless numbers of people in town in agreement in prayer for the healing of that poor girl. There were religious visions galore where God himself supposedly proclaimed that his healing power was about to be demonstrated to his glory. Trance mediums, preachers, psychics, church members, everyone was seeing the same visions, receiving the same messages of healing and deliverance, everyone was in agreement in prayer. And...? Nothing. A poor young girl's tragic, senseless, and untimely death.

And a voice that spoke aloud to me...the truth.

Whose was the voice? Was it God's? The Devil's? An Angel's? The Reaper himself? Some other Higher Being or Power of which we're not even aware? I have absolutely no clue. I've never been given even a glimmer of information or explanation.

It was a distinctly deep male voice. Pleasant sounding. Nonthreatening. Very matter-of-fact. Unemotional, but not unsympathetic.

If the being to whom this voice belonged was so all-knowing in this situation, could not that prowess have been turned to healing for the poor girl? Why additional suffering leading to an untimely death?

"She is mine. She will be with me within two week's time."

All I know is that I learned that day that no matter what we see, no matter what visions we receive, no matter how fervently we agree in prayer...most often we don't get to call the shots. And whatever reasons these higher powers have for certain things, it seems that many times our feelings and wishes aren't taken into consideration.

The experience put a dent in my faith that's lasted to this day, and I still have no good explanation for the voice.

If you sincerely believe in the spiritual realm, and you sincerely attempt to practice your spiritual beliefs for the good of others, you're sure gonna get handed some lumps and bruises.

The experience was just the beginning of my awakening. And sometimes I wish it were one that I'd never had.

In Memoriam. Rest in Peace.

CHAPTER 8

My Dad Died

IN A BOOK of poetry I wrote, the lines from a poem about my father's life and death reads:

Reality took off her silken glove
And slapped me in the face

Then the Reaper caught my eye
And gave my Dad embrace.

The lines reference a further coming of age, a deepening of maturity, and the realization of the harshness of life.

My dad seemed so rugged, so indestructible, that it was inconceivable to me that he would die. But die he did, and it really rattled me. I was learning first-hand how easily my world—a world that I had assumed would remain fairly stable—could fall apart.

It would take me awhile for it to sink in: he's really gone.

In addition to my psychic gifts and explorations I had become an ordained minister. When my father began to fail and was basically bedfast he made a request of me: that I would be the one to preach his funeral. I promised him that I would.

When the time came I kept my promise to him. It was one of the hardest things I've ever done. It necessitated that I control my emotions, hold in all of my grief, and comfort and guide family members and friends while performing a dignified service for my father.

I succeeded; and when all was said and done I allowed myself to break down, cry and grieve.

My father's funeral was the first I had ever conducted. But it would not be the last.

Before my dad died I had married and had fathered a daughter. As I said I had also become an ordained minister, and after my father had died I became an associate pastor of a small church. The backstage machinations of organized religion repulsed me, and I would soon leave the church and organized religion altogether. But before I did, a family friend requested that I would come and minister to his dying wife.

She was a patient at one of the prominent local nursing homes and was running out of time. He told me that he had repeatedly asked the pastor of their church—where they had faithfully attended for a number of years—to come and minister to her, but he had never visited her…not even once, according to her husband.

So I went to see her. Her husband was there when I came to visit and I held her hand and gave her some biblical guidance and comfort and told her that when she crossed over that the angels and deceased friends and family members would be there to meet her, which I honestly believed. It comforted her greatly, and I prayed with her and her husband, and I visited her a few more times.

Her husband would tell me repeatedly how grateful he was to me, and that he couldn't understand why the pastor from their own church would promise to come and visit her and never would. It kind of blew my mind, too.

Anyway, one evening I was preaching the service at the church where I was associate pastor when the woman who lived next door to the church and was also its caretaker and housekeeper came walking briskly through the doors of the church. She stopped at the pew where the pastor was sitting and handed him a piece of paper.

He arose and said, "John, I'm sorry to interrupt you. Folks, give us a minute please. I'll explain shortly."

He brought the note to me where I stood in the pulpit. The man had called: "My wife is dying. Can John please come?"

The pastor told me to go as quickly as I could and that he would take over the service and explain to our small congregation what had happened.

I hopped into my car and drove as rapidly as I could to the nursing home, raced to her room, and her husband looked up with tears in his eyes and told me how thankful he was that I had come, and that he was sorry for disturbing my sermon but that no one else had come to help them and comfort them.

I told him it was perfectly fine, not to worry about the sermon, that the pastor had covered it and that my being here with them in her final moments was what mattered the most. I stated that I considered it an honor that he would call me.

I held her hand, and his, and prayed. She gasped the death rattle a few times and then, as I held her hand, her spirit left her body. We said another prayer and just stood quietly for a moment.

There was an overwhelming sensation of peace and a powerful spiritual presence in that room that everyone noticed, nurses included.

And then, (too little too late; too bad) in came the pastor of their church, to a cold reception from the husband and a feeling of disdain from me though I tried hard to be professional. Their pastor tried to make a big show of being there as a powerful spiritual presence and as their comforting spiritual leader, but the husband sure wasn't buying it and apparently neither were the nurses.

I received a call from the widower a day or so later asking me if I would preach his wife's funeral. I told him that I didn't think that would be appropriate since I wasn't their pastor. I didn't want to be unprofessional and step on toes, regardless of the circumstances. He then asked me if I would preach at the funeral if the pastor of their church would give me equal time, and I told him that if he would discuss it with his pastor and the man agreed that I would attend and preach half of the service.

Surprisingly, his pastor agreed, and I spoke first at graveside and then took my seat.

Their pastor got up to speak and the first words out of his mouth were how blessed he had been to visit with them and comfort them as members of his congregation and how wonderful it had been to minister to the man's sick and dying wife.

The widower leaned forward in his seat in the rows of chairs that were at graveside, his eyes wide as saucers as he caught my eye and stared at me. I shook my head slightly, gave a tight-lipped little smile and discreetly brought my finger to my lips to indicate, "Shhh."

He shook his head in disbelief at his pastor's duplicity, I nodded slightly to indicate that I understood, and he leaned back in his chair for the rest of the service.

It was just such shenanigans as these that had disgusted me with organized religion, but the straw that broke the camel's back was a reprise of events that I'd experienced in my youth at the prayer group conducted by my mother at my old home.

Pretty, hot-looking women with great bodies and great legs would come to church dressed ever more scantily. Their makeup grew more pronounced. Their skirts and dresses got shorter and shorter. Their hose or stockings got markedly sexier. And their heels got higher.

They would choose a seat on the front pew directly in front of the pulpit and cross and uncross their legs slowly and suggestively while I preached.

My wife and I were in the throes of a failing relationship and it all proved to be too much.

I left the church and organized religion and never looked back.

CHAPTER 9

Losing My Religion

I HAD BECOME mad at God. I had dedicated myself to the church for nearly a decade, studying the Bible, praying, ministering...and what I learned in all of those years was that it was Hallelujah Sunday, same old Monday.

We would whip ourselves into an emotional religious frenzy Sunday morning and Sunday night, proclaiming ourselves blessed and healed and sanctified and then if you were to meet anyone from the congregation on Monday morning it would be business as usual. Same old health problems, same old issues, same old life everyone else was leading, church member or not.

You know what? In all of my church years and all my years as an ordained minister and eventual associate pastor of a small church, I never saw one legitimate miracle inside the church. There were plenty of supernatural events that continued to happen outside the church (which I just relabeled as gifts of the spirit), but I can't recall one legitimate supernatural event inside the church. Not any of them. Ever.

And don't even get me started about the god-awful phony crusades and giant healing and miracle meetings held by some of the big-name evangelists. I attended a few and found them to be so blatantly phony and predatory that it sickened me.

As I got older, my eyes opened wider, and I saw such greed, such duplicity, and so many sexual shenanigans inside the church that it drove me away. I could not participate with good conscience in an institution that preached holiness while flinging sinfulness in the face of God in the confines of the church building itself.

I saw such blatant and vulgar flirtation among church members that it turned my stomach, and again, I'm no prude. But damn. Openly rubbing yourself against another while your spouse is standing right there watching, and you proclaim yourself to be godly?

Well, I had had enough. I was through with the lies and deceits of the church, and I was also mad at and tired of the spiritual and paranormal in general. Desperately needed help and guidance was too spotty and unreliable, if it came at all, regardless of its supposed source. I tried to turn my back on it all. But it didn't turn its back on me.

I divorced, and my sister was also divorced, and we both moved back into the old family home. Ostensibly to help care for our mother who was in rapidly failing health, but I think we both needed some shelter from the storm, a place without too much pressure or responsibility while we tried to make some sense of our lives and sort things out for ourselves.

And I learned that my mother was as untrustworthy as ever, but I had learned how to keep my distance and safeguard myself against her machinations.

While still married and before I moved back into the family home I'd adopted a large red female Doberman, Elsa. She was a hundred pounds of pure muscle and incredibly strong, as well as wonderfully loving, and extremely intelligent. God, I loved that dog, and she loved me. She was a true and faithful companion, and we spent many happy hours together. She had exceptional endurance and begged to go running with me. I asked my vet about it and he said that I could start her on short runs and gradually build her up, all the while watching her for signs of distress. I allowed her to run with me while on a leash and she progressed to the point that she covered five miles easily and barely had to pant. I, on the other hand, because of my asthma and COPD, was puffing like a steam engine by the time we finished our runs.

I tried my best to ignore the paranormal goings-on, which continued in spite of my indifference, and in spite of the fact that people continued to seek me out for readings and spiritual guidance, just as they had in the church when I was a practicing ordained minister.

I returned to school, made new friends, and in spite of all of my severe health issues I pushed myself as never before, running up to 14 miles at a time; playing tennis; hiking; lifting weights; practicing my martial arts; continuing to put in miles on my racing bicycle; regularly swimming up to a quarter of a mile nonstop; and performing calisthenics: When I'd wake up at four or five a.m. I did fifty to one hundred leg lifts and fifty to one hundred sit-ups while still in bed before I went out for my early morning run.

I became a party animal, leaving school early in the afternoon, usually getting in another physical workout, and then hitting my favorite bars until they closed. I'd be up at 4 or 5 a.m. and do it all over again. I had hit my stride physically in spite of my health issues and I was going to become as fit as I could for as long as I could in order to stave off as many problems of old age as possible.

Ironically, all of my board certified specialists told me that my vigorous physical activity is probably what contributed to my eventual health downfalls.

For my entire life, the paranormal was there. Along the way I worked at full-time jobs and part-time jobs, depending on the circumstances, but I always provided readings and counseling for others. There were times in my life when I'd work eight hours a day, and then come home and spend six to eight hours providing readings for clients.

But during the phase when I turned my back on all things spiritual (or tried to) I attempted to distance myself from clients and those seeking counseling as much as possible. But the Other Side wouldn't let me. They were politely, gradually persistent, trying to get me to acknowledge my gifts and to continue my service to others.

Why? I would rail...why should I exercise such a gift that would allow me to see that people were going to die and not be able to do anything about it? Why should I continue to immerse myself in a spiritual realm that mysteriously healed some sufferers completely and yet allowed others to die when those who died were as steadfast in their beliefs and as committed to seeking healing as anyone else?

One night near Christmas I drove to the outskirts of town along a deserted highway. I parked, got out of my car, looked up into the beautiful clear dark sky sprinkled with a stunning array of stars, and I shook my fist at those heavens and yelled at it, demanding an answer, demanding knowledge, demanding help both for myself and others.

There was no sign; no answer; no manifestation.

I shook my head. "I thought so," I muttered, and got back into my car and drove home.

CHAPTER **10**

Back to the Egg

MY SISTER AND I had invented a game. The game was played thusly: one of us would attempt to scare the other so badly that we would cause them to have a stroke. As a consequence of my sister and me frequently playing horrific pranks on each other I slept with my bedroom door locked, so I was rather amazed to awaken to what could be presumed to be an intruder in my home.

Shortly after my heavenward-directed tirade I was sound asleep one night, resting comfortably in what had been my father's old bed, when I was suddenly awakened by the feeling of a presence standing behind me.

I was lying on my side and the presence was standing by the side of the bed to which my back was turned.

Now I was completely wide awake. My martial arts training kicked in and I prepared myself to roll over and launch an instantaneous and devastating attack on this invader. I took a breath and started to roll over to confront this person and discovered that I could not move. My eyes were wide open and moving...I could look around my room and see details, even in the dark, thanks to light streaming in my windows from various bright streetlights and outside lights that neighbors left on at night. My roller shades dimmed the external light but didn't dampen it completely.

My breathing was normal.

I could even wiggle my fingers and toes, but I couldn't move my torso, my head, or my limbs. And then it finally dawned on me.

"Who are you?" I whispered into the darkness.

Someone very gently and with a feeling of great tenderness and compassion laid their hand on my shoulder, and then gave my shoulder a squeeze, holding on for a good five seconds or so. And then they let go.

The split second that their hand left my shoulder I was instantly able to move and I flipped over in bed and turned on the light on my nightstand, but of course that was all in vain for there was no one in the flesh in my bedroom, and all of my doors and windows were closed and securely locked, just as I left them when I went to bed.

I sat there for a moment, whispered thanks to whoever it was that had come to visit with me and encourage me, turned out the light and went back to sleep.

Maybe someone heard me after all when I was out on that deserted highway raving at the night sky.

After that encounter I began to open myself up again. I hadn't received any great cosmic answers or revelations, but I thought that to be okay. I would at least exercise the amount of knowledge that I had, and maybe more would be given to me.

Was the loving hand on my shoulder my father's? Some other deceased relative's? A touch from a spirit guide or a guardian angel? I never did get a definitive sense of things one way or the other, but I did occasionally receive signs that I knew beyond a shadow of a doubt were from my father, usually manifesting to me in times of illness or stress.

One of my father's nightly rituals was to take Mentholatum brand salve and rub some on his eyelids, closing each eyelid individually and in turn smearing a generous gob on it, and then he would smear some on his nose and under his nostrils, on his lips, and as a grand finale he would actually put a little gob in his mouth and allow it to dissolve and slide down his throat.

I don't know what the folks at the Mentholatum company would say to that; they'd probably be aghast and I'm sure there's got to be a warning somewhere on the jar against internal consumption. I certainly don't recommend that you try it.

But my father never seemed to suffer any ill effects and he lived to be a ripe old age. And when he died they didn't list the cause as "Mentholatum poisoning."

But, needless to say, the smell from this nightly ritual would permeate the house.

When I moved back home I occupied my father's former bedroom and, being the clean freak I am, I set about dusting, scrubbing, sweeping, mopping, and disinfecting everything. This was not to get rid of the Mentholatum smell, for by that time there was none, not even on his mattress.

And I don't just like things clean and fresh…there has to be an aroma, a sweet fragrance of some kind perfuming the air in my environment such as the aromas from scented candles or burning incense.

So it was naturally with some amazement that I was occasionally overwhelmed by a strong aroma of Mentholatum, so strong that it was as if someone had opened a large jar directly underneath my nose. The scent of the Mentholatum was so forceful that it would completely overpower the aroma of whatever scented candle or incense I might be burning.

Sometimes the Mentholatum smell was isolated to one particular spot in dad's old bedroom; if you moved away from that one spot you immediately ceased to smell the fragrance. When you moved back to that spot, the aroma would again be in evidence, and then suddenly disappear.

Other times the scent would be so overpowering that my mother, who was practically bedfast by this time in the bedroom next to dad's (where he had lain bedfast for a brief time before he died) would ask me if I were ill and if I was rubbing myself down with a mentholated salve.

My sister would frequently comment on the overpowering aroma, and it occasionally became so strong that her little dogs would sniff the air and rub at their eyes.

I would always say, "Hi dad, I love you and miss you."

We all began to accept the aromatic manifestations as evidence that my father was contacting us from beyond the grave.

The aroma continued off and on for the remainder of my years at the old house, coming especially in times of crisis or ill health. When I finally left the old home for good I never smelled it again.

In spite of pretty strong anecdotal evidence that my mother may have occasionally been poisoning us, she was a terrific cook. She had a knack for it that she inherited from her mother, and we enjoyed many a delicious meal until she became too ill to man the cookstove anymore. At that point, my sister took over, and she was also an extremely talented cook.

I was still quite the party animal and when I came in late at night I walked up the sidewalk to our back porch, which had two windows with views into the kitchen, and I caught a glimpse of my sister either at the cookstove or walking back and forth in the kitchen from the cookstove to the sink.

What was strange about these sightings was not the fact that they occurred late at night. They were strange experiences because the only light on in the kitchen emanated from the night-light we kept turned on. The overhead light was never on.

The first time it happened I presumed that my sister had cooked a late night snack and had turned the overhead light off in preparation for grabbing her food and heading back into her apartment.

By the time I unlocked the back door and entered the house she was no longer in the kitchen, and the door which led into her apartment was closed.

I didn't think much about it the first time it happened, but when it began to recur on a regular basis I knew something wasn't quite right.

I'd come in and there would be a dark figure that was about the shape and size of my sister hovering about the cookstove, and occasionally walking back and forth in the kitchen, again only to the light from the night-light.

I finally wised up and instead of going to the back door I went to my sister's apartment and looked into her windows.

Lo and behold, there she would be, watching TV.

While standing outside and watching my sister through her window I'd glance back toward the kitchen windows of the main house and see the dark figure still moving back and forth in the kitchen.

Ah, I thought to myself, a hungry ghost.

The manifestation continued to occur when I came in late at night.

And then...I would be in bed, either watching TV with the sound down low, or maybe even drifting off to sleep, and I'd hear the door to my sister's apartment open, quick footsteps go into the kitchen, cabinets open and close, sometimes the rattle of dishes and glasses, and occasionally I'd even hear the door to the refrigerator open and close. The footsteps would retreat, and the apartment door would close, and I merely thought that my sister was coming in for a late night snack. (By this time, my mother was bedfast; it couldn't be her.)

My mother sometimes even heard the sounds in the kitchen from her bedroom and hollered out to my sister one night to please bring her something from the kitchen. The sounds from the kitchen immediately quieted and did not resume.

My mother called once more to my sister, but...nothing.

My mother asked my sister the next day if she had not heard her call out during the previous night when she was in the kitchen.

My sister looked strangely at my mother and told her that she had not been in the kitchen last night.

"But I heard you," my mother said.

"So did I, sis. I've heard you come in during the night several different times and open and close the cabinets and sometimes the fridge."

My sister looked at my mother and me like we were both nuts and informed us that she hadn't been going into the kitchen that late at night.

We told her about the experiences, and we all chalked it up to paranormal manifestations.

One night I heard the apartment door open and the footsteps enter the kitchen. I got quickly and quietly out of bed, went to my door, unlocked it, and opened it a crack to look into the kitchen. The cabinet doors had been opening and closing and there was some dish noise until I opened my door and peeped out. The moment I did it stopped. There was no one in the flesh there; just the hungry ghost.

I told you that the footsteps I experienced as a child had moved inside our old home, and the hungry ghost's audible footsteps were only one example.

As time went by, and before my mother became completely bedfast and could still make it to the dining room table and her chair in the living room, we held small dinner parties, inviting anywhere between five and ten guests, and my sister would cook.

My sister was a pie cooking fiend...she turned out some of the most amazing pies I've ever tasted. One of our friends who we invited to the dinner parties tasted my sister's pies (my sister usually baked two or three different kinds of pie for each party) and offered to set her up in the pie-making business.

Our friend had space already equipped as a commercial kitchen. She was going to sell it but when she discovered how good the pies were she offered to pay my sister a salary and open up the space to the public, selling my sister's pies and other baked goods.

My sister politely declined, explaining to our friend that it was fun to bake occasionally for family and friends, but that if she had to do it on a daily basis for work it would take all of the fun out of the experience and turn it into drudgery.

Anyway, the folks who attended our dinner parties for the most part believed in the paranormal, and many had experienced their own strange manifestations.

Usually, after the meal was eaten and the last bites of pie were consumed we all adjourned to the living room to semi-recreate the prayer group of old, encouraging supernatural manifestations to come forth, praying for those who were ill or needed other assistance, etc.

At one such dinner party a family friend brought a guest. We were all sitting around the dining table enjoying the last remnants of the meal and engaging in small talk before going into the living room. At this point, we all heard what our guest heard but none of us said anything.

Our guest began to lean back in his chair and try to look into the kitchen and farther into the house. He kept doing this and then he finally started counting heads at the table, pointing to each of us with his finger while moving his lips to take a silent head count.

Our friend noticed the guest's behavior and asked him, "What in the world are you doing?"

The man replied that he was trying to figure out who was walking around in the kitchen and in the other parts of the house. "Who haven't I met, and why didn't they come to eat with us?"

We asked him why he asked such a question and he replied, "Why, because of the footsteps. Hasn't everyone heard the footsteps? Who is it? Does someone else live here?"

No, we assured him, everyone who lived in the house was present at the table and there were no other guests.

"Then who—" he began, stammering, "then who's making the sounds of footsteps? Who's walking around..." and he let it trail off as his eyes widened and he looked at the friend who had brought him. "No," the man said.

"Yes," his friend told him, and we explained that it was quite common to hear footsteps in the house all the time, that the spirits had always been quite active in that manner.

It scared the guest so badly that he would not walk anywhere in our house by himself, and we all had a good laugh at his expense, as I'm sure the spirits must have too.

And years later after I sold my old home and left town for good, the footsteps came with me.

My mother had always provided food for the birds, and they came by the hundreds in the morning when she put out their seed. We bought bird seed in 50-pound bags and went through them quickly. When my mother was no longer able to carry the food outside, my sister and I took over the chore.

Among the birds that came to enjoy the food were cardinals, blue jays, grackles, crows, sparrows, pigeons, and doves. Most of the other birds would eat and fly away, going about their daily routines and roosting elsewhere, then showing up the following morning for breakfast. The doves, however, would eat and then decide it wasn't a bad place to hang around until the next meal. After all, we had a couple of bird baths that we kept filled with fresh water, and there were plenty of trees in which to roost. In the evening I could go outside and walk around, looking up into the trees to see dozens and dozens of doves settling in, some already sleeping with their cute little eyes closed.

One day I found a dead dove on our property. I picked it up and examined it carefully. Physically it appeared perfectly normal and intact. It looked like the bird had died of old age or some disease, or a heart attack perhaps.

I told it not to worry, that I would give it a dignified place of rest. I dug a hole by our old garage, gently placed the dove into it, covered it up with dirt and then I placed a large stone on the grave, not only as a marker but to keep any errant animals from digging the carcass up. I said a little prayer for the bird's spirit, and then went about my business.

After performing that little ritual for the deceased dove, word must have spread somehow. Any dove that must have sensed it was soon to die came to our property to do it, and I found and buried each and every one, giving them a little grave marker and saying a prayer for them.

It got bizarre: one day I was futzing around in the yard and I spied a dove perched on a low branch of a tree, not more than a few feet off the ground. When my big Doberman, Elsa, came close to the tree, which grew right by the chain link of her pen, the dove wouldn't even budge.

That bumfuzzled me so I edged closer to investigate. The dove was clutching the branch with its eyes closed. I thought maybe it was asleep, although with all of the goings-on around the little bird it would surely have had to be one sound sleeper.

I ventured close enough to gently touch it, and my astonishment grew: the little bird was stiff. It had closed its eyes and died right there, holding onto that branch.

I gently removed it and buried it too.

I guess I had become the Bird Whisperer.

I had the craziest dream one night. In the dream this man gave me his name and told me that he was deceased and needed to get a message through to his family that lived on a farm in a nearby small town.

He told me their names and the name of the town (there happened to be a complete section of that small town's phone directory in our local phone book, including the complete phone directories for several surrounding small towns).

As the dream ended he began yelling: "You must call them. You must tell them. You have to tell them about this dream. Tell them that I told you. You must do this for me. It's urgent."

And then I woke up.

The first thing I did was to grab the phone book and look in the directory for that town; and lo and behold, there were the names the man had given me in the dream. Now what do I do? I wondered. I could envision the call going something like this: "Hi. You don't know me, but I'm John Russell and I'm a psychic. I frequently have dreams and visions and dead people come to visit me all the time and tell me things, and so-and-so came to me in a dream and told me to give you this message."

And I could imagine the typical West Texas response: "Who in the hell is this? Is this some kind of prank? Is this a joke of some sort? Where are you? If I get my hands on you…"

So, I waited a day or so before I mustered up the courage to call the number. I had my spiel all memorized and ready to go, as well as a profound apology ready if my call angered them.

I took a deep breath and called the number. The call connected and the phone rang and rang and rang…no one answered, and it never went to voice mail and there was no answering machine either.

After I hung up, out of curiosity I called the operator and asked if she would please check on the number for me, to see if it was a valid number and still in service. She assured me that it was.

Well, it was a farming community. It wouldn't be unusual for people to work in the fields and not carry any sort of mobile phone with them. So I decided to try my call in the evening when there may be someone in from the fields, or someone making supper.

I tried again. Nothing.

I tried several more times, and no matter what time of day or night I called, the phone rang and rang and rang and no one ever answered and there was never any voice mail or answering machine message.

I finally said a verbal apology to the man on the Other Side who had come to me in my dream and told him that I was sorry, but that I'd tried and tried and tried and I did not know what else to do.

He never came back to me anymore, and I finally just let it go, although I did think off and on how strange it was.

And then, many years later, when I was living in New York, I had another similar circumstance happen…not through a dream, but through a voice mail that was left on my phone. That story will come later.

One morning early, before 9 a.m., I was driving a delivery truck around town for a company that I worked for during the day.

At the time I was dating this gorgeous, flashy gal who had a distinctive appearance and a distinctive car.

As I was driving eastbound on a major street through the city I saw her car coming westbound. I thought it odd for her to be out running errands so early, so as the car approached me I double-checked to make sure that it was her, and there was no doubt that it was. Our lanes were side by side as we passed each other, and we were on a long curve that gave me extra time to look at her and her car.

I saw her face clearly. And she stared straight ahead as she drove, with one of the oddest expressions on her face that I'd ever seen on any human being.

I honked and waved but she didn't respond. She didn't even look my way as she passed me; she just kept on driving by with that strange look on her face.

I immediately grabbed the phone in the truck to call her home number and leave a message that I had seen her on such-and-such a street and so early in the morning for her, and what in the world was she doing out and about, and why hadn't she paid attention when I honked and waved back at me?

I nearly dropped the phone when she answered after the first two rings.

I stammered: "What in the world are you doing home?"

"Well, John…that's a stupid question. Where else would I be but home? I live here, don't I?"

I couldn't speak for a moment, and then I finally told her that I had just witnessed her doppelgänger. I had to continue with my work so we agreed that we'd discuss it later, but neither one of us could assign any significance to the sighting at the time.

I have seen several doppelgängers in my lifetime, but that was the most startling occurrence yet.

Things would sometimes appear or disappear around the house. One of the most dramatic occurrences happened one afternoon after I had taken a nap.

I used to wear earrings, and I had a fairly large gold skull and crossed-bones earring that I was exceptionally fond of. I decided to take a nap in the early afternoon, so I took the earring out of my ear and placed it onto a white side table that was next to the recliner in which I took my nap. The gold earring against the bright white of the table stuck out like the proverbial sore thumb, and I must mention that there were no other items on the side table, only the gold earring.

As usual my bedroom was locked up tight against the possibility that my sister would try to scare me enough to cause that fatal stroke, so there was no way that anyone could have entered my bedroom without my knowledge.

I had a nice long nap, and as I awoke I noticed that it was still a beautiful, sunny day. I stretched and decided I wanted to eat Mexican food at my favorite restaurant. I looked over at my side table and started to grab the gold earring, which was lying in the center of the table where I had placed it earlier.

No, I decided, I would wear a different earring instead. I got out of my recliner, walked around the bed to the nightstand and opened the drawer in which I kept my earring collection, selected one, and then for some odd reason I decided that I would wear the gold earring after all. I closed the drawer, walked back around the bed to my recliner and the side table…and the earring had vanished.

In the short amount of time that it had taken me to walk around my bed and back someone on the Other Side had swiped my earring.

In later years, while I was on vacation, during the night someone on the Other Side swiped another of my earrings that had been lying in plain sight on a counter.

Neither of those earrings ever returned. But I did receive an unusual gift from the Other Side, which I still have to this day. That story will come in a moment, but first a story about a most unusual manifestation. I guess you could call it a gift, but more accurately it was a literal return from beyond the grave.

I told you that my sister and I had both moved back home. She had a couple of small dogs, and one of the little dogs was always sickly and in poor health, though he played quite vigorously on a good day.

My sister was a store manager and arose early to go to work, bringing her little dogs in and putting them in bed with my mother, who adored the little critters. They would lie on the bed with her most of the day, and it was good company for my mother who was growing increasingly bedfast.

My sister had provided one of her old robes as a blanket for the dogs to lie on when they were on the floor, and the sickly dog especially loved that robe. He would scratch around and hide his toys in it, pawing at it until he had managed to roll the robe up into a ball, and then he took delight in unrolling it to get his toys out.

One of his absolute favorite toys was a large green plastic frog with a squeaker in it. He had played with the frog so much that it was grungy, and its look made it easy to distinguish from other similar toys. It was quite distinctive in appearance.

I was still attending our university at the time. One day I had either come home early in the afternoon from school or had the day off, I really don't remember, but I made myself a sandwich and was sitting in the dining room, enjoying my food, and looking out the windows, just letting my mind wander. I remember I was in good spirits. The day had a pleasant energy to it, and I was enjoying myself.

I heard the sound of one of the dogs jumping down from my mother's bed and I turned my head to look over my right shoulder and saw that it was the sickly little dog who had come down the hallway and was entering the dining room. He would walk behind me while making his way to the kitchen for a bite of food or a drink of water. As he walked behind my chair I turned my head to gaze over my left shoulder and watch him as he walked by. When I turned my head to the left a woman bent down so as to place her face within a few feet of mine.

I jumped up, overturning my chair in the process—which hit the floor with a loud clatter, causing the little dog to skitter away into the kitchen—and I threw my sandwich.

My mother asked what happened and I replied that it was okay, I had just seen a ghost and it had startled me.

She asked if the ghost had a message, and I lied and said that there was no message, though as a matter of fact, there was. But if I told her the contents of that message her heart would break.

What had transpired during the brief ghostly visitation was this: The woman appeared so clearly to me that I remember her to this day. She was smiling happily; she was pretty; she had short, dark hair styled in kind of a bob; she wore a long-sleeved light-colored blouse and a straight, formfitting skirt that hit about her knees, and was tan or light brown in color. She had on hose, and wore flat shoes, like loafers.

And in a few seconds she telepathically communicated to me that the little dog was terminal (regular vet visits had intimated as much and I think we all had our suspicions) and that she was following him around periodically to check on him and that she would be there when he died to cross him over. Wow.

And sure enough it wasn't more than a week or so later that the little dog died in his sleep.

We always buried our animals on our property, and so we dug a hole in the back yard for the little dog. We watched as my sister began to wrap his tiny body in the robe he had loved so much, and she placed his green frog squeak toy next to his body. She finished folding and winding the robe tightly around his body until it became a small parcel not much bigger than the little dog himself.

We buried him, packed the dirt down tightly, and I placed a large flat stone on the dirt just until it began to congeal enough that it would be hard for critters to attempt to dig through.

Flash forward and the grass had regrown over the little dog's grave. The lawn was so smooth and perfect that there was absolutely nothing to indicate the whereabouts of the grave; if you didn't know that the little dog had been buried in that spot there was certainly nothing to give it away. The only way we knew the exact location was that we had been careful to note its distance from the clothesline pole and in relation to the back fence and a few other markers.

One day I had been out on foot for some reason, and as I walked by Elsa's pen I stopped to say hi to her and then continued to walk up our driveway. I always parked my old car in a different driveway, a short old gravel driveway that led into our dilapidated wooden garage, which was a short distance over from the main driveway. My sister was at work, so I had a clear field of view all the way up the driveway and into the back yard. It was a sunny day, late in the afternoon, the temperature was pleasant, and I was enjoying my slow stroll up the driveway when something sitting on the lawn underneath the clotheslines caught my eye.

I walked over that way to see what it was and sitting on the top of the little dog's grave was his green frog squeaky toy.

The ground was not disturbed in the least; the lawn was pristine; there had been no digging, no evidence of any kind of disturbance of the soil whatsoever. And yet here sat that frog toy, so distinctive in appearance, having somehow been teleported through multiple layers of cloth robe and several feet of densely packed soil.

I couldn't believe my eyes. I bent down and picked it up to examine it. Sure enough, it was the little dog's favorite toy with which he had been buried.

I knelt down and ran my hand over the grass, even probing the ground with my fingers. I even pulled on the grass all around and over the grave to see if it had been dug up and then replaced. Nope. Everything was solid and absolutely undisturbed.

I said a word of greeting to the little dog, gave thanks to the Powers That Be for such a mighty supernatural demonstration, and then I sat the frog toy on the steps leading up to my sister's apartment in a spot so prominent that I knew she couldn't miss it when she came home. Then I went inside and told my mother what had happened, and I waited.

I heard my sister's car pull into the driveway and the engine turn off. She seemed to be sitting in the car a little longer than usual, and I knew why. She had seen the frog sitting on the porch step and was probably doubting her sanity or at the least wondering if she was hallucinating.

Finally I heard her car door open and shut, and her apartment door open and close, and the sound of her footsteps as she came racing into the house, holding the frog in her hand.

I had made my way into my mother's bedroom when I heard my sister coming, and she raced into the bedroom and looked at me, holding the frog up and shaking it toward me.

"Did you see this?" she asked, astonishment and disbelief evident in her tone of voice.

"Yep."

She was speechless for a moment. When she found her voice again she asked, "Where in god's name did you find it?"

And I told her how I had walked up the driveway and had seen it sitting on the lawn on top of the little dog's grave.

She was gobsmacked. She even had to go and examine the gravesite for herself in order to ascertain that it was indeed undisturbed and that a little miracle had taken place.

She kept the frog for a few days and then told me that she wanted to give it to Elsa to play with, that it was a way of keeping the memory alive, and so we gave it to Elsa, and she played with it until it finally wore out.

CHAPTER **11**

A Belated Christmas Miracle

THIS STORY, OF all of the fantastic ones I've told you, is perhaps the most meaningful, for it was a life-or-death situation, unbeknownst to us in the family.

Our home was heated entirely with natural gas. We had a gas hot water heater, a gas range (cookstove) and oven, and gas floor furnaces and space heaters. And, as you can imagine in a home where people love to cook, the range and oven received especially heavy use.

As our Texas winters include days that can be quite cold, we also made liberal use of our wall heaters, floor furnaces, and three gas space heaters.

Not only were there the constant pilot lights burning on all of the gas appliances and also the open flames of our heaters and furnaces, but ever since I was a child my mother and I had loved to burn candles and sometimes incense.

So there was always a fire of some type, an open flame of some type, burning in our home.

Over the years as my family's finances had declined my parents had been unable to pay for even normal and routine maintenance, so they began to severely neglect repair and maintenance on our old home, including the gas appliances, furnaces, heaters, and the plumbing also.

Oddly enough the electrical never gave us any problems, but the plumbing sprang a new leak almost weekly it seemed. And there were

71

occasional problems with the aging floor furnaces which necessitated shutting them both down since parts to repair them were practically unavailable.

We occasionally detected an odor in the house that we assumed was from the leaking plumbing pipes underneath the house's crawl space. It seemed like nearly everything underneath the house leaked and on the slim budget we could manage to scrape together, we couldn't stay on top of all of the problems. We assumed the odor might occasionally be sewer gas.

All our other gas appliances seemed to work fine, and we experienced no difficulties with them year after year, using our space heaters and wall heaters at least daily when the temperature dropped, and of course during a particularly cold spell sometimes they would run for days straight, 24 hours a day, without ever being turned off.

And all those years, six of them, that my sister and I lived at home and took care of my mother, we continued to use our heaters, the range, the oven, and of course I continued to enjoy the pleasure of lighting candles and incense, almost daily.

And for all of those six years we smelled that odor.

As I mentioned before, when mom could no longer cook, sis took over the chore and cooked delicious meals almost every day. We kept the house toasty warm for mom, because as she aged and the illnesses with which she was beset took their toll, she was often chilly.

Lots of open flames in that old house...day after day, month after month, year after year.

Well, when mom died, just a few days before Christmas, I got in the habit of lowering or turning off much of the heat when I went to work, and I'd fire up all the heaters when I got home to take the chill off the big old house, and then turn down or turn off all but a few that I really needed to sustain warmth at a comfortable level for me.

One such day I'd walked home from work, entered the chilly house, and methodically made my rounds lighting all the heaters, including the wall heater in my bathroom.

Sis was still at work, and I was rather tired, so I sat down in my recliner to watch the evening news on TV.

Of my bedroom's windows, one double set faced west, my bed being directly underneath them, and the setting sun streaming through the branches cast shifting abstract patterns on my bed's comforter as the branches swayed gently in the breeze.

I saw a flickering in my peripheral vision, toward my bathroom, but there was an absorbing news story on TV and thinking I was merely seeing the sun cast more patterns as it shifted position I ignored it at first.

Then the flickering became brighter and more noticeable, and I pulled my attention away from the TV to look and I was horrified at what I saw.

The wall heater was burning…and so was a large tongue of flame about six to eight inches long, shooting out of what I discovered was a crack in the old heater's gas inlet pipe.

I sat there stunned for a moment, then it dawned on me: my God, the entire house could blow sky high at any moment.

I jumped up and raced into the bathroom to make sure my eyes weren't deceiving me, and I could clearly see the crack in the inlet pipe, illuminated as it was by the flame shooting out of it.

I stood there a moment, frozen with indecision, praying aloud. Then I reached down and turned the heater's handle to the off position. The flame from within the heater's grates went out.

The tongue of flame continued to burn.

I ran to the phone and called our gas company's emergency number, told them the situation and asked what I should do.

They asked if I knew where the gas meter was located outside, and I told them yes. They instructed me to get a wrench and to go turn the main gas valve off on the meter.

Then they informed me that they'd dispatch some emergency vehicles from the gas company immediately. I thanked them, hung up, found my wrench, ran outside, and turned the valve off on the gas meter.

I ran back inside the house and looked in my bathroom, half expecting the flame—for some mysterious reason—to still be burning and I breathed a sigh of relief when I saw it was out.

About that time my sister called and asked me if I wanted her to stop and pick up some fried chicken for dinner on her way home from work. I told her that her call and her offer could not have been timelier, and then I explained what had happened. She inquired as to whether I was okay or not, and I told her yes, that I'd been incredibly lucky and hadn't even been burned. Nor had the fire somehow spread to the dry old walls of our house.

She gave thanks, and I told her I'd go into detail on the story when she got home.

I went and turned our dining room light on, pushing in the old button-style on-off switch, the kind that makes a large spark that's highly visible in the darkness when you turn the lights on as there's some delay between pushing the old switch and the lights coming on a brief second later—plenty of time to see the spark caused by pushing the button in. And yes, it made a spark this time when I turned it on.

I walked to the windows that faced the back yard, looked out, and saw a truck from the gas company pull into the alley behind our house.

I opened the back door and walked out to the alley to meet the serviceman.

He asked what had happened and when I gave him all of the details he gave me a sort of funny look which I really didn't understand, and then he went to his truck and got a small, hand-held meter that detected gas in the atmosphere, indicating the presence of gas both with a needle on a gauge and an audible alarm.

As soon as he turned the meter on, still standing in the alleyway, the needle on the meter pegged, and the alarm squealed loudly.

"What in the world?" he muttered to himself, checking the meter's adjustment controls. He shook his head, turned it off, back on, and the meter pegged, and the alarm squealed again.

"Well, this damn thing," he said, turning it off and on again, whacking it on its side and again staring in disbelief at the squealing little machine.

"Where's your gas meter?" he asked. I pointed a few feet behind us to the alley, where the meter sat in the alley just on the other side of our chain link fence. The evening had progressed into one of twilight's darker stages by the time he'd arrived, and he hadn't seen it when he pulled up.

He walked over to the gas meter, turned the gas detection meter on, and again it squealed and pegged the needle.

"You turned the gas off, didn't you?"

I assured him that I had.

"This darn thing. This little meter must be malfunctioning, because it's detecting gas all in your yard, all in the air out here, and we're a good thirty or forty feet from your house."

I shrugged, and he walked the length of the buried gas line all the way to the house, occasionally turning the meter on. It behaved exactly as before.

"I sure don't understand this," he said, shaking his head.

He turned the meter off and walked up onto the back porch, letting out a whoop. "Man, you smell that gas?" I had left the door open, and you could smell a whiff of gas coming through the screened door.

His eyes were large behind his glasses; I inhaled through my nose to sniff the air and shrugged. Occasionally we'd smell an odor that we identified with our leaky plumbing problems, and we let it go at that. I hadn't even really smelled any gas odor that night when I'd been lighting all the heaters.

"You can't smell that? Man, that's strong."

We entered the house and he turned on his meter again, where it repeated its prior performances.

With that he looked at me wide-eyed. "This meter's not wrong. The house and your whole yard outside is filled with gas. Get doors and windows open, now."

I complied while he helped, and finally he stepped out the front door onto our front porch, shaking his head and complaining that the fumes were getting to him. "This hasn't bothered you?" he asked incredulously.

I assured him I hadn't smelled it at all earlier and could only catch a faint whiff of what seemed to be knocking him over.

We let the house air out a good little bit, and he walked back in and turned on the meter. It acted the same as before.

"There's something wrong here," he said, "because we've had the house open long enough to clear out all this gas."

He walked from room to room, the little instrument squealing and screaming as before, shaking his head as he went. When he saw the crack in the inlet pipe into the bathroom heater, he again stared up at me and shook his head.

"You know why this meter keeps going off?" he asked.

When I told him I didn't, he supplied the reason. It was spine-chilling.

"Everything in this house is leaking gas. The gas meter in the alley is leaking gas even though it's supposed to be turned off. The main gas pipe into the house is leaking gas its entire length. We're going to have to pull the meter and cap the line, and you'll have to call a plumber to come out tomorrow and fix the lines. Then we'll come and inspect and install a new meter. Your old one is even the wrong size for this house, by the way. It should be much larger."

We walked outside together, and another gas company truck pulled up in the alley behind his.

We walked together to meet the new arrival, and when the man asked what had happened the other employee told him the story, while I stood by and listened.

The second man's eyes grew wide as he heard this tale, and when the first man finished the second man asked, "How badly was he burned?"

"He wasn't." Turning to me he pointed and said "That's him. Right there."

The man stared at me in disbelief, then at the first man, then back at me, as if we were pulling some huge prank on him.

"Come on, I'll show you," the first man said, and we all walked into the house together. He periodically turned the meter on and off, with the accompanying squeal each time.

When the second man glimpsed the crack in the pipe of the heater, he stared in wide-eyed disbelief at his partner, and both shook their heads.

"I don't want to be gruesome," the first man began, "but you people shouldn't even be alive."

His companion nodded. "Really. I'm like him, I'm not trying to be scary or gruesome, but man, there should be a hole here the size of Detroit, and this house, and all you folks, should have been blown sky-high long ago."

The seriousness of what I had lived through began to dawn on me.

My sister arrived home, and the two men hastened to tell her the story, and just what a perilous life we had been living and had somehow managed to survive. Of course my sister's eyes widened as mine had, and she and I exchanged nervous glances.

"This is a Christmas miracle," the first man said, the second man vigorously nodding in agreement. "I believe in miracles after this night. And you people should too. I know it's a little late for Christmas," (this event having transpired in January) "but you've received your Christmas miracle, albeit a bit late. If you don't believe in guardian angels, you should now. I have seen a miracle this night."

As sis brought our chicken in to eat, the men had to marvel further that I'd used the phone, which produces electrical activity, and turned on that sparking wall switch with our house so full of gas, and had not been, again, blown to Kingdom Come.

They pulled the meter and capped the line, reminding us frequently what a miracle this was and how lucky we were. We agreed. Stunned, we agreed.

None of us at the time knew exactly how large a miracle had occurred that night and had been occurring for years.

Guardian angels, indeed.

My sister was home the next morning to wait on the plumbers, and I took off for work. The tale she had for me when I came home for lunch was the most amazing of all.

In testing for gas leaks the plumbers pumped the gas lines full of air, attached a meter with a mercury gauge in it (kind of like a blood pressure gauge I guess) and opened the valve into the gas lines to see how fast the mercury dropped.

I don't understand all the technical details and may not have gotten them exactly right, but that's the gist of it—you can call a plumber and they'll tell you what they do.

Anyway, when they opened the valve and began to pump air into the gas lines, the mercury gauge would immediately plummet to zero.

The meter leaked. The entire underground gas line going into the house leaked. All of the appliances leaked. And there were leaks in the gas pipes underneath the house in the crawl space and no doubt there had been lots of built up gas underneath the house in days, months, and years gone by.

In all, the plumbers found seventeen major leaks.

Seventeen.

In the yard. In the house. Under the house. The gas meter itself.

The plumbers repeated the same story, that we should have been blown sky-high many years ago, and the neighborhood reduced to rubble from the massive blast.

They were as wide-eyed and incredulous as the men from the gas company had been.

We understood why.

For they were calling it a miracle too.

That's why I believe in Guardian Angels, and that God directly intervenes in the lives of people. Sometimes in ways that are simply unbelievable. But true.

My repeated thank-yous to Him and His angels are woefully and pathetically inadequate in the face of what we experienced.

But again and again and again: "Thank you. Thank you so very, very much."

Sometime after our miraculous rescue from a certain and hellish death, my sister moved into her own apartment in a complex in our town, and I stayed at the old house, by myself.

Sis's apartment she rented was all electric, by the way; and she made it a point to tell me that as we shared a sort of grim humor about the fact. But with the gas system repaired I was once again comfortable and felt secure in my old home.

Sis and I adjusted to mom's death each in our own different ways.

But the impact of her death remained strong with us.

After my sister moved out into her own place, it seemed like much of the energy and joy disappeared from the old home. It was in severe disrepair, and my salary wasn't nearly sufficient to begin reparation. I cleaned and patched and repaired to the best of my ability, and set about working in the yard, but it was obvious the old home had seen its better days.

Plus I was tired, as was my sister...my mother's years of sickness and her having been bedfast at the end took a toll on us emotionally, physically, financially...in all ways.

So my sister and I each began to adjust to the shock of having lost our last parent, and the fact that the loss had been under difficult and trying circumstances.

Of course paranormal phenomena continued in my life, and both I and the old home were magnets for it just as much as before mom died. But things kind of took on new meaning now, as I continued to grow and mature and probe the deep mysteries and pains of life, finding out that we all face the inevitable, and that many times, no matter how we search or hope or pray, there are no answers forthcoming.

Season faded into season as I spent a little over two years by myself at the old home, alone, but not lonely.

I had Elsa. I had spiritual contact. I had freedom to come in from work and sit on the back porch, watch the sun set, and mull life over. In peace and in quiet.

Although I missed my mom and my sister, I think the time that my sister and I had apart to allow ourselves to heal with no responsibilities to anyone but ourselves was a positive experience in both of our lives.

And—hot dog—I learned to cook.

Up until that time, either mom or sis had always cooked, and the few attempts I made actually resulted in their requesting that I stay out of the kitchen.

When my sister moved out it suddenly dawned on me that I was going to starve. Well, no, not actually, but I realized that it would be too expensive for me to eat out all the time, and I would quickly grow tired of sandwiches. What to do?

As if on divine cue a set of recipe cards appeared in the mail one day. There was a subscription offer: if I enjoyed the sample recipes I could subscribe and every few weeks or so a new set of recipes would be sent to me. I was saved. I could learn how to cook and take care of myself and also feed my daughter when we had our weekends and other times together.

Suddenly it was as if some new talent had grown within me, and I began to prepare my own delicious meals, all from scratch, and I also taught myself to bake. I became completely and totally self-sufficient. I had an old car I'd inherited from my mother with the house, along with the debts of the estate and other responsibilities and I knew I would eventually have to sell my old home in order to take care of certain legal obligations.

But for the time being I was free.

I had a car, so I could get around as I pleased. I had a roof over my head. A spacious roof. I could play whatever music I wanted to, as loud as I wanted to, whenever I wanted to. I could run around the house naked if I desired. I turned the huge living room into my painting studio and would paint indoors when the weather was inclement. I cooked. I baked…pumpkin bread and banana-nut bread and pies and cakes. Elsa periodically got the run of the house. I worked in the yard and tried to bring back some of mom's beautiful hybrid irises that had been so neglected over the years.

I envisioned exactly how I would fix the old house up if I were to win the lottery. But that never happened.

I knew I would have to move someday. The old house was falling down around me, coming apart at the seams.

And then I met the woman who was to become my second wife, and I fell in love again. She had an apartment. I sold my old, dilapidated home and moved in with her as a matter of survival: my old house was becoming uninhabitable.

Her apartment complex didn't allow large dogs, and so I was also forced to part with, not only my beloved old home, but my beloved Elsa, one of the best friends and companions I had ever known.

I prayed to God almighty to grant me any conceivable out so that I could keep Elsa and manage to stay afloat, but this became the only path available to me, and my heart was broken by having to find Elsa a loving family with whom to live. I've never gotten over losing her.

My second wife and I experienced many paranormal manifestations together. We had our ups and downs as all couples do, but you could have knocked me over with a feather when she came home one day at lunch and informed me that she was divorcing me. No, I didn't foresee it coming; I'm psychic…not God.

What made this particularly difficult for me to deal with was that my health problems had progressed to the point that I was mostly bedfast many days; I had no job; precious little financial resources; and no place to live. I became homeless overnight. It was one of the most frightening times of my entire life.

But, thanks to dear friends and constant help from the Other Side, I survived, and went on to eventually recover and lead a good life once again. Actually, in time, I began to lead a life that would be the best I had ever experienced.

Oh…I promised you the story of the unusual gift I received from the Other Side. Here it is.

I'm an artist, which makes me excessively visually oriented to begin with, so I'm always exceptionally careful with my food preparation, and I notice all the colors, textures, and so forth as I'm preparing meals.

Cooking is as much a visual treat for me as it is for the olfactory senses and the palate.

As I prepared the ingredients for this particular batch of chili, I examined each ingredient for quality and purity as I added it. There's no way anything the size of a BB could have made it into the chili pot without me seeing it.

I cooked the batch up, and it was delicious. I ladled the leftovers into a bowl, which of course gave me the opportunity for another visual examination as the chili poured from the ladle into the bowl.

Nothing was amiss in my chili. I would have noticed any anomaly, anything strange or out of the ordinary.

The next day I spooned a healthy serving from the bowl in the refrigerator into a smaller bowl, which I placed in the microwave to heat up.

I paused the microwave a couple of times in the heating process to remove the bowl and stir the chili thoroughly, and again there was nothing amiss.

When the chili was good and hot I brought the bowl to the table, and as I sat down to eat I decided a large helping of grated cheese would be the coup de grâce for such a delicious meal. I grated some cheese onto my chili, and then stirred some of the cheese in so it would partially melt from the chili's heat, which meant that I once again had an opportunity to look at this bowl of food as I stirred it thoroughly, and again I saw nothing amiss. I grated a small amount more cheese on top, then sat down to eat and enjoy.

It was delicious, and as I ate, I periodically stirred the contents of the bowl, gazing in appreciation at this wonderful culinary treat and thanking God for the goodness of food.

I was just about to take another bite when the phone rang. The phone in the bedroom was equipped with an answering machine with which I could screen calls before taking them, and I got up,

A Belated Christmas Miracle

walked maybe fifteen feet or so to our bedroom door, and stood there to listen and see if it was a call I needed to take. I didn't want to interrupt my meal if I didn't have to.

The phone stopped ringing on the second ring, and there had been no message left. I shrugged, turned around and walked back to the table, to my bowl of chili.

I hadn't been away from my bowl for more than thirty seconds or so. I was home alone. There was no one else there who could have tampered with my food when I went to check the phone.

I picked up my spoon, and looked down in my bowl of chili, and in the exact spot where I had just looked before the phone rang and from which I had been about to take a bite there was something black and shiny just under the surface of the liquid.

At first I thought "mushroom," for I frequently love to use various kinds of mushrooms in my cooking, and chili is not sacrosanct to me...I'll dump anything in that tastes good, including beans.

But then I remembered that I hadn't used mushrooms...

"An olive, a black olive," I thought, but quickly dismissed that idea as well; I hadn't put any olives into my chili either.

I spooned the object out.

It was a small chunk of wood.

A chunk of wood had mysteriously appeared in my chili when I went to monitor the answering machine.

There was no possible way for a chunk of wood that size to have made it unscathed through a meat grinder, and it was ground beef that I used in my chili.

Also, through each attentive and careful step of preparation, and all the visually monitored stirrings afterwards, I would have seen this piece of wood sticking out like a stop sign on a field of yellow daisies.

I picked the wood out of the spoon with my fingers and dried it off on my napkin.

It looked just like a piece of old barn wood and one end, only one end, was charred black as if that portion had been in a fire or had been burnt by a saw cut.

In spite of knowing that there was no place earthly this chunk of wood could have come from, I examined every cabinet door in the kitchen for a piece of missing wood, which I knew of course would be futile, for the cabinets in the apartment were made from an entirely different type of wood, and all the cabinetry was in good shape.

I also marveled at the timing of the appearance of the wood in my bowl of chili, for it surely must have been a paranormal power making the phone ring to divert my attention away from my bowl long enough for this surprise to appear.

I thanked my spirit visitors aloud for my "gift," laid it down on the table beside me, and finished my bowl of chili.

There are paranormal photographs I've lost in moves, and some artifacts which have gone by the wayside, but I still hold on to this piece of wood.

Maybe whoever took my earring that time decided to bring me something back in return.

All I know is that my already strong psychic powers were increasing greatly with the appearance of each new paranormal manifestation, so I welcomed each and every one as a sign of my growing connection with the invisible realm.

CHAPTER **12**

A Major Friend

BILL WAS THE friend who took me into his home when I became homeless as a result of the divorce from my second wife.

He was a retired Air Force Major and had also done work involving top secret clearances, including some work for the NSA. This led to a few interesting conversations and provided fuel for animated discussions involving, among other things, UFOs, but he never revealed any classified information. He kept his security oath sacred and intact until his dying day.

Bill and I had been friends for a number of years, and I was so overwhelmed with gratitude that he would open up his home to me, providing me with a room in his house, feeding me until my financial situation improved, driving me around in his truck when I needed to run errands, and much more. He crossed over several years ago, and lord do I miss him.

Anyway Bill told me one time, "John, I believe you have a real gift, a genuine gift. I believe in everything you do. But, if you see, feel, hear, or experience anything in my home…I don't want to hear about it." The paranormal scared Bill, and so I always asked my guys, the retinue of spirit beings that followed me around, to behave and not act out when Bill was home.

"Don't move things, don't make noises, don't manifest…just behave and be quiet until Bill leaves to run errands or something and then you can make all of the noise you want or do whatever you want. Just not when Bill's home."

And for the most part the guys behaved themselves.

My health issues varied while I stayed with Bill. Some days I could walk from his house up to the corner of the block, catch the city bus, ride it into town and walk around a good little bit running errands. Other days I felt so lousy I barely came out of my room.

What was really bizarre to me during this time was that I could still manifest a gift that I had been able to manifest before: healing of others. Healthwise I just couldn't seem to do a darn thing for myself.

Once when I felt good and rode the bus, I interacted with one of the other regular bus passengers who had undergone back surgery and was wearing a brace and walking with the help of a cane. He, like most people I knew who had undergone back surgery, was not much—if any—better off, and he was in horrific pain. When he got on the bus I'd wave him over to the seat in front of mine and we'd chat a bit before he turned around for the rest of the ride. Likewise if he were to be on the bus first I would take the seat behind his when I could. I did that purposefully. When he wasn't paying attention I would place my hands close to his seat back at about the level of his lower back and begin transmitting healing energy to him. I did this for as long as I could, every time we rode together.

Within a few days of such treatments he zipped onto the bus one morning without his brace, still using his cane, but much spryer of step. Everybody on the bus commented on how well he was doing, and the man said his doctor had told him that for some odd reason his healing began to accelerate and that he had never seen a patient recover from back surgery as quickly as this man was doing. I was delighted.

Another awesome experience occurred at a bar Bill and I loved to frequent.

One of the waitresses came over to say hi to us while we sat at the bar and she talked about the cold sore (or fever blister) she had on her lip. "My god, it's like I have a goiter." she said. And it was. The sore was only a day or so old, meaning that it had days to go, maybe a week or more—even with medication—before it healed; and it was huge. It was one of the largest cold sores I had ever seen…big, angry-looking, and inflamed.

I asked her if she would mind if I tried something. I explained that I wanted to zap some energy into the cold sore and see what happened. She readily agreed, and right there at the bar in this busy restaurant I began to transmit healing energy into her cold sore through my forefinger, which I pointed directly at the sore from maybe a half inch away.

I stopped and asked her if she felt anything and she said yes that the sore began to tingle strongly. She asked me what I had done, and I just laughed and said, "It's an old Indian trick I learned." She shook her head and went about her business, and next day Bill and I were sitting at the bar again and she ran over to me and said, "Look." The sore was totally, completely gone. There was not a trace of it on her lip.

I told her I was glad. So was she, if not more than a little flabbergasted.

Bill said, "That's some weird shit, John."

I laughed and we enjoyed our libations.

I could heal people's headaches instantly. My ex once burned her finger badly from a hot glue gun accident and it was blistered and red and swollen. I transmitted healing energy to it and later that day the burn was almost gone and the next day her finger was completely normal. And yet I couldn't seem to help myself.

One year while staying with Bill I felt particularly frisky and in July of 1998 I decided I would go to Alien Encounter 98 in Roswell, New Mexico and perform psychic readings there. I paid my vendor's fee, rented a car, and drove to Roswell.

While there I had two amazing experiences. One, I got to see Stanton Friedman lecture in person.

Two, I had an "Alien Encounter" of my very own while waiting for the Roswell UFO Museum to open.

Early one morning I was standing on the sidewalk in front of the Roswell International UFO Museum and Research Center, waiting for it to open, when this woman came walking down the sidewalk and for some reason we struck up a conversation.

I explained to her that I was waiting for the UFO Museum to open, and she asked me if I had been to the museum before. I told her no, that as a matter of fact this was my first time to visit Roswell even though I was born in New Mexico. She asked if I was on vacation and I explained to her that I was a psychic and that I was giving readings at Alien Encounter 98.

We conversed a little longer and then her next statement shocked me so much I'm sure I struggled to keep my mouth from hanging open.

"When we were kids," she said, "my brother and I were playing outside, and we saw the UFO come over and then crash off in the distance."

I'm sure my eyes had widened. I was in awe. She continued.

"We could tell it was in distress. We weren't surprised that it went down. And we knew beyond a shadow of a doubt what we saw. It wasn't a helicopter; it wasn't a plane; it wasn't a weather balloon or a blimp; it was a UFO. A flying saucer."

Wow.

We talked a little longer and she also told me that many of the townspeople had been threatened if they talked about the UFO, especially those who had actually seen it, as she and her brother had. The clear implication—or in reality, threat—was that if a person talked about what they had seen, their bones, as well as those of family members, would be found out in the desert.

She said that there were still some townspeople who were afraid after all these years, and then she suddenly whipped her head left and right several times, looking up and down the street, and abruptly stated, "I've said too much. I shouldn't have talked to you. I'm sorry, goodbye."

And she hurried off down the street, leaving me dumbfounded

and standing alone once again in front of the museum as I waited for it to open.

I saw some interesting exhibits that day, but nothing was as interesting as what that woman told me.

This woman's experience certainly goes a long way toward explaining why witnesses to UFO incidents may be reluctant to come forward and testify.

Another reason a great deal of secrecy surrounds these events is that those in the military and the government who swear oaths of secrecy really do honor those oaths.

An example was my good buddy Bill…Major Bill.

We'd be well into our cups and sometimes conversations would turn to UFOs, military technologies, things Bill had seen when he was briefly a pilot, and he would begin to tell me some astounding things and then suddenly censor himself, even when the info wasn't classified.

"Ah. I've said too much. That's all I'm gonna say, and forget you heard that. No more. I'm not going to discuss it anymore so don't ask."

So people really do take their oaths of secrecy quite seriously.

After my divorce and while I was staying with Bill I tested the waters by starting to date again.

As I was getting on my feet financially another friend of mine had set me up with a computer and Internet service. I met a woman online and we agreed to meet for drinks.

I was my usual West Texas good old boy charming self, just as suave and debonair as could be…what's not to like? And this lady was really charming. Pretty, well educated, good sense of humor, great personality…and dang it, wouldn't you know…not a bit of romantic chemistry between us.

But we honestly did hit it off as friends, and we'd occasionally talk on the phone or e-mail or meet for drinks. I really liked her, and I believe she held the same friendship feelings toward me.

One New Year's Eve we met at one of my favorite watering holes for a drink. It was around nine and she asked what my plans were for the evening. I told her that after she left I would have another drink or two, head home, and go to bed.

"You're not even going to see the old one out and the new one in?" she asked.

"Nope. It'll be there in the morning," I laughed. "What are your plans?"

She informed me that she was going to meet some girlfriends at one of their houses and they would have snacks and wine and sit, talk and laugh and stay up to see the old one out and the new one in.

She got up to go, gave me a kiss, we wished each other well, and then I stopped her.

"Hey. I'm going to send a ghost home with you."

Now she knew what I did, and she was a believer, but that brought her up short.

"What?" she laughed.

"I'm going to send a ghost home with you."

"Yeah, okay, whatever."

"Listen, I'm not kidding. I'm going to send a ghost home with you. You'll see."

She laughed and hugged me, and we bade each other goodnight. I had another drink or two and then went home, went to bed and to sleep.

I should mention that I have performed psychic readings professionally since the age of 18, and in full-time spurts and spells, but with my friend bankrolling me and helping me, I began to advertise consistently and I threw my hat into the ring to read full time and not work at anything else.

I was beginning to get a fairly good roster of clients and people would call me at all hours of the day and night, so when I went to sleep I'd turn my computer off and turn the ringer on my phone off so that I could get some rest. In the morning I'd fire everything up and begin to handle messages and e-mails and make appointments.

Well, the following morning, New Year's Day, I got up and turned on my computer and checked my e-mails. There were a few from my friend, in all caps. There was also one or two phone messages from her as well. I read the e-mails and listened to her messages and this is what had transpired.

She went to her friend's house and met with her other girlfriends there. They congregated in the kitchen/dining area and sat around the dining table and chatted, snacked, and drank. Her friend had one of those multi-tiered wire baskets hanging from the ceiling, the kind that you would put fruit in: bananas, oranges, etc. Now keep in mind this was on New Year's Eve. It was cold outside. Her friend's house was closed up tight...no open windows or doors that would produce drafts or anything like that.

The wire baskets were not under or in the path of any heating/cooling vents.

As they sat around the table and talked, my friend observed from the corner of her eye, the baskets begin to swing slightly. Oh my god, she thought, but she didn't say anything, and she even tried not to look, but the basket began to swing in an increasingly large arc until one of the other women took notice and commented on it.

The woman whose house it was stood up and said, "What in the world?" and went over and put her hands on the basket to stop it from swinging.

They all wondered what could have caused the phenomenon and speculated on the possibility of vibrations from passing cars or planes to who knew what. My friend said she rolled her eyes and refused to say anything.

Everyone commented on how odd it was, but they all sat and resumed their conversations and my friend said that from the corner of her eye she saw the baskets begin to swing again, but this time, as they all watched, the arc grew so large that the baskets were swinging back and forth in an arc that was one to two feet.

By now everyone was flabbergasted, and she unintentionally blurted aloud, "That John and his damn ghost."

That got everyone's attention and they asked her what in the world she meant. "Who's John? What ghost?" And then she had to explain what had transpired previously that evening.

They got the basket stopped, she gave the explanation, and everyone had a high old time the rest of the evening because of that experience and the subsequent conversation it provoked.

I was also skilled in psychometry: divination of facts concerning an object or its owner through contact with or proximity to the object. Bill and I were once again sitting at the bar of one of our favorite watering holes when a female acquaintance of ours came in, and we invited her to sit with us.

We both commented on the beautiful ring she was wearing, and as she started to tell us about it I stopped her.

"Give me the ring."

She took it off her finger and handed it to me. I rubbed the ring for a few moments and then I said, "You bought this ring in Austin, from a street vendor with a cart. It was a bright sunny day."

"Oh my god," she said, "yes. That's absolutely right."

Bill looked over at me. "Again, John: that's some weird shit."

I laughed, and we enjoyed our drinks together.

Bill would occasionally leave me in charge of his home while he took a vacation to see old military buddies. On one such occasion I was sitting in his backyard, enjoying a beautiful day.

Over the top of the section of his fence which ran parallel to the alley behind his home I spied some objects floating in the air over the middle of the alley. They traveled toward me and as they got closer I could see that they were shaped like bubbles.

They were grouped closely together, and there was a large one about four to six inches in diameter, another only a little smaller, and then one more still smaller than the other two. I couldn't help but think to myself, "Papa, mama, and baby."

They were perfectly round. And their appearance was difficult to describe. They were kind of white, but not. Nearly translucent, but not. They didn't seem to reflect the sunlight, but rather to emanate their own, perhaps from within.

They didn't float down the alley blown by a breeze, for it was completely still with not a leaf stirring on a tree anywhere in sight. They moved under their own power, and they gave me the impression that they were intelligent. They would stop, start, move closer, and then finally, as a group, they dove down into a neighbor's yard directly across the alley from me. Even if I had been able to peek over the top of Bill's fence it wouldn't have done me any good, for the neighbors had a privacy fence as tall as Bill's.

I tried to send some communication to the manifestation and ask it to return or perhaps to even come and visit me, but I never saw them again. Nor have I seen anything that even remotely resembled them since.

My dear old friend, Bill. How forever grateful I will be that you gave me a home when I so desperately needed one, and that you made it a home for me. I miss you and love you. Thank you.

CHAPTER **13**

New York, New York

WHILE I WAS staying with Bill I met a woman on the Web through Yahoo's personals: Marjorie.

We hit it off and began to correspond via e-mails, and that progressed to phone calls, and then she came to meet me face-to-face when I traveled to Alien Encounter 98 in Roswell.

Long story short we kept up our correspondence and our phone calls and then she came to San Angelo and met my friends. Shortly thereafter I went to New York and met her friends, and the rest is history. We've been together for 22 years now as of this writing.

I thanked Bill for his hospitality, said farewell to my San Angelo friends and my old hometown, and moved to New York. Cornwall, to be precise, in upstate New York.

Marjorie had a beautiful 200-year-old home there, and I fell in love with it and with New York itself.

And Marjorie was right at home with my psychic gift and the guys' shenanigans, as she had friends who were psychics and she had experienced some paranormal manifestations herself.

When I first moved to New York my health again declined rapidly and I couldn't do much at all.

Then, as one of my weird health conditions is prone to do periodically, I experienced a remission, and I was able to walk a surprisingly good distance again and even to resume my beloved gardening.

And that was an especially good thing, for I was contacted one day out of the blue by Atlas Media in New York City. They were working on a proposed series for The History Channel, with the working title of Psychic History and they were looking for psychic talent to interview.

They requested that I send them an audition tape, a pre-recorded video audition that an actor or would-be talent submits to the casting director or creative team.

Marjorie and I decided that one of the best places to film the audition would be in the attic of our old home, which was the site of spectacular paranormal phenomena.

She would get the camera rolling, I would start to introduce myself, but then we'd both crack up laughing. After several such misfires we finally got a decent take and sent the video tape off to Atlas. I guess they liked what they saw, because they contacted me for a screen test. A screen test is a filmed audition in which an actor demonstrates their suitability for a role in a film or television show. And that's how I met TV producer, writer, and editor Jim Mullen, who was working for Atlas Media at the time.

We filmed my audition, and my demonstration of my psychic prowess was convincing enough that we went to production with the pilot episode of Psychic History, during which I would psychically investigate mysteries of the past, specifically the assassination of President Abraham Lincoln.

What an incredible experience it was. We filmed at Ford's Theatre, where President Lincoln had been assassinated; the Petersen House (President Abraham Lincoln died there after being shot the previous evening at Ford's Theatre, located across the street.); the Surratt House Museum (Mary Elizabeth Jenkins Surratt was an American boarding house owner in Washington D.C. in 1865 who was convicted of taking part in the conspiracy to assassinate U.S. President Abraham Lincoln. Sentenced to death, she was hanged and became the first woman executed by the U.S. federal government.); the Dr. Samuel A. Mudd House Museum (Dr. Mudd was the southern Maryland doctor who set the leg of John Wilkes Booth the morning after the assassination of

Abraham Lincoln.); and finally we went to the location of John Wilkes Booth's demise.

Because we had the cachet of both Atlas Media Corporation and The History Channel many doors opened up for us that would have otherwise remained closed, so we were welcomed at these historic landmarks.

I had never been on camera before, so I was nervous, overawed, and excited, but also tremendously grateful to be given this opportunity to appear in a meaningful series (I signed a five-year contract) about the supernatural.

We had an excellent and talented crew in the field: Jim Mullen, producer; Jacqueline (Jac) Gares, co-producer; and cameraman/cinematographer Sam Henriques. And me, trying to learn on the fly and figure it out as we filmed. Everyone was so kind and also so generous with their time and knowledge, helping me to understand the technical details and how to present myself on camera.

They must have done something right, for later on when I was approached by other production companies who had seen a rough of my pilot as an audition tape, other producers couldn't believe it was the first time I had been on camera, and they all said I was a natural.

Before I get into the juicy details of the events that transpired at the locations where we filmed, let me dispel a misconception that some of you may hold: filming a TV episode is not glamorous; it is hard work. 12-hour days were the norm, and sometimes we worked 16 and 18-hour days.

I also had to get used to being referred to as the "talent."

Now, I'm an old West Texas boy, and in my day and time I was raised so that if I parked in a grocery store parking lot and I saw a woman carrying grocery sacks in her arms as I was entering the store, it was just a matter of course from my upbringing that I would approach the woman, tell her that I would carry the sacks for her, and then walk her to her car and load her groceries into her car.

So the morning that we all assembled in Manhattan to load the van and begin our journey to these incredible historic sites in D.C.

and Maryland I went to pick up one of the cameras so that I could help the crew load the van. I learned two things: first, I was admonished for attempting to do any type of manual labor or physical exertion to help the crew. "The talent doesn't do those things," Jim explained. "What if you hurt yourself lifting a camera, for example, and then we had to delay or even cancel filming? Also you could work up a sweat and we don't want to film you looking all sweaty." Got it.

The second thing I learned: those cameras you see hoisting up on their shoulders and carrying around to film shows and events? They're heavy.

We were filming in the van as we drove to D.C. and while I was on camera Jim asked me to say my name and then come up with a tagline, something that we could use in subsequent episodes as a reiterated phrase that would come to be identified with me and the show.

Sometimes I'm not known for thinking fast on my feet; I desperately searched my mind for something meaningful, and as the camera rolled all I could come up with was, "I'm John Russell. Let's go find some ghosts."

It horrifies me to this day, but Jim still finds it to be funny.

Part of the concept of our series was that I would never know the exact locations of where we were going to film; this eliminated any possibility of research on my part beforehand. What we wanted the viewer to understand from that concept was that I was not allowed to research a location before we went. Therefore any psychic knowledge about the location and whatever events had transpired there would be shown to be genuine and not something I learned before traveling to that site.

The crew even took it to the extremes sometimes: As I'm writing this I just now got off the phone after speaking with Sam, our cameraman, who told me that he believes he still has some stills of me blindfolded in the seat of the van as we were on our way to a different location.

What would make the experience even more enthralling for me is the fact that I was a terribly poor history student. I actually knew precious little about our country's history, possessing virtually no information beyond the most obvious facts that were common knowledge to everyone (Who killed Lincoln? John Wilkes Booth.). And I'm glad I wasn't a history buff. That way there were less memories rattling around in my head competing with my psychic gift.

For our first location I was deposited on the street with a camera tracking me and given a piece of paper, on which was written: Please go to 511 10th Street NW (in Washington, D.C.). When I got there I saw that we were at Ford's Theatre, the site of President Lincoln's assassination. I mounted the steps, the camera following me, and my psychic powers kicked in. I turned and looked at everybody in the crew and said, "Watch, the door's going to be locked."

"Oh, no," I was assured, "they know we're coming. It's all been arranged and they're expecting us."

I finished climbing the steps, grabbed the door handle and pulled to open it, and Ford's Theater was locked up tighter than a drum. This tickled me no end for some reason, and Jim called and told them that we were outside with the talent and the camera crew, and they came, unlocked the door and let us in.

My god…what a huge energy I felt when I stepped into that theatre. Years can go by. Furnishings can come and go, be replaced, or be duplicated. A building can be scrubbed and cleaned and painted or even refurbished and refreshed or restored. But you can never scrub away the psychic impressions left behind by such a monumental tragedy.

And I've learned something interesting over the years: a duplicate object that mimics the original will give me as accurate a reading as the original itself would have. Perhaps it's because in the final analysis I'm not reading the object itself, but the energy, the memory it left behind. (Here we could wade into some deep, esoteric territory and speculate that replacement objects may somehow over time cosmically absorb some of the authentic energy from the location in which they're placed. But that's a subject for another book, perhaps.)

For example, I never realized until today's phone call, while talking to Sam, that for the most part the furnishings in the Petersen House were recreations.

For me at the time that made no difference in either the strength or the accuracy and validity of my psychic impressions. At the time of my investigation, the events replayed themselves for me as if it were a movie I had watched just the day before instead of an event that occurred nearly 150 years ago—regardless of whether the furnishings were or were not the real historical article.

But anyway...Ford's Theatre. I climbed the stairs to the second floor on my way to the upper-tier, and the theatre boxes that include the Presidential Box where Lincoln was shot.

Midway up the stairs I encountered a warm and pretty female spirit in period dress or period costume: She wore a long, billowing dress; a large decorative hat; and carried a parasol.

I initially thought that the apparition may have been one of the actresses at the theatre from long ago. I got an o-l-l-y name, and I specifically said it's a name like Polly or Molly. But we would learn that there was a surprising match for the name Molly; a Lincoln historian informed us that Lincoln frequently referred to his wife, Mary, as... Molly.

I made it to the second floor and took a seat in the front row of the theatre, facing the stage and the Presidential Box. It was well known that Lincoln had premonitions. Tuning in my psychic senses I became aware that Lincoln had a premonition that the assassination attempt was going to occur, that he had these feelings of impending doom and this certain dread, and when Booth threw open the door to the Presidential Box in that split second of time Lincoln realized, "This is it." He knew that his premonition had been correct.

In doing some quick research online as I write this, it's said that Lincoln suffered both death threats and assassination attempts from the beginning of his Presidency, with one source placing the count of received death threats at over 10,000. Either Lincoln didn't take the threats seriously, or he was just one ballsy son of a gun. Maybe he became a little too cavalier about his safety as the years went by and he continued to remain unharmed. At any rate I could not discern any fear in Lincoln, even though he realized what was about to happen. In his last few seconds of conscious life on this earth he embodied this quote attributed to him: "I do the very best I know how—the very best I can; and I mean to keep on doing so until the end."

I will tell you one thing further that I have discerned now that I didn't really perceive at the time of my investigation in Ford's Theatre: Lincoln was furious with extreme rage at the cowardly act that Booth perpetrated on him. Lincoln took hours to die and as his spirit hovered between this side and the next I get the feeling that his rage grew, and that he came to realize what a wide-reaching and sinister plot had actually been hatched against him, and against America. For it wasn't just Lincoln that was the target; there was a plot in hand to disrupt the government and take down America and cause chaos. More assassinations other than Lincoln's had also been planned, I learned at the time of my investigation. Some had apparently been thwarted. But I picked up on some of the co-conspirators and saw that they had become faint of heart and had withdrawn themselves from the plot.

One such spirit appeared to me from around the corner of the doorway leading into the Presidential Box (sometimes called the State Box) and beckoned me to follow. I was able to describe the ghostly figure I saw and later to pick him out in a photograph of some of the co-conspirators. He was one of the ones who had decided that things had gone too far and that he didn't want to be a part of the process any longer. He was terrified of being caught and may even have tried to dissuade others who were in on the plot.

Standing and looking through the window into the Presidential Box I psychically gleaned that after Booth shot the president and then leaped down to the stage that he yelled something at the audience, but the words he yelled were confusing to me and I couldn't figure them out. Some historians agree that it was reported that Booth yelled *"Sic semper tyrannis,"* which is a Latin phrase meaning "thus always to tyrants."

Standing there at the doorway looking into the Presidential Box where Lincoln had been shot I was suddenly overwhelmed with sorrow at the senseless violence. I felt so sad I just wanted to leave.

One of the growing bits of psychic awareness that came over me as I stood in the theatre was that there were many people involved in the assassination plot, something that was confirmed by one of our Lincoln experts who stated: "While it was Booth's hand that held the gun, there were many fingers on the trigger."

And I picked up on another chilling fact: in the audience that night, sitting in one of the back rows, was someone who was not only in on the plot but was there as a kind of overseer to ensure that Booth performed as desired. This person might have even been there as a kind of back-up assassin, or to order other would-be assassins who were planted in the theatre into action should Booth's attempt fail. It was a sinister revelation.

Going into the theatre's museum I noticed a door with a hole drilled in it, representing the door to the Presidential Box, and the statement was that Booth may have drilled the hole in the door in order to be able to spy into the Box from outside, enabling him to plan on when he would burst in and shoot the president. My psychic senses told me that no, Booth did not drill the hole himself, but had a co-conspirator or sympathizer do it for him, a workman or someone else who wouldn't arouse suspicion by being in the theatre that day.

A revelation provided by Frank Ford, a descendant of theatre owner John Ford, supports my psychic vision. Frank Ford claims that Booth did not drill the hole, that it was done at the instruction of Harry Ford (theatre treasurer and brother of John Ford) who instructed one of the theatre's carpenters to make the hole in the door, ostensibly so that the President's bodyguard could look through the hole to keep an eye on the President. (One wonders where the bodyguard was when Booth took his post at the peephole.)

From Ford's Theatre we went across the street to the Petersen House, where Lincoln was taken after he was shot.

I psychically discerned, as you might expect, that the house was a hive of activity during the night as people of importance came and went and tried to keep a steady hand on the government.

But the most amazing thing to me was that I could almost physically hear poor Mrs. Lincoln as she wailed inconsolably throughout the night. I explained that this was not the occasional sobbing outburst you'd ordinarily expect, but a near constant crying out that sometimes bordered on hysteria and screaming, something that was later confirmed to us by historians.

And Lincoln? He resigned himself to his passage to the Other Side and crossed over in a quiet and dignified manner.

I was asked, both in Ford's Theatre and in the Petersen House, if at this stage of things I felt that Booth had felt any remorse, guilt, or shame. I replied no, that he was proud of what he did and totally unrepentant.

And from there we left behind Ford's Theatre and the Petersen House and continued on the trail of the assassin.

CHAPTER **14**

On the Trail of the Assassin

WE FOLLOWED THE trail that John Wilkes Booth took when he fled Washington, D.C. on horseback.

Somewhere along the way—or possibly, as many believe happened when Booth vaulted over the rail of the Presidential Box and landed on the stage at Ford's Theatre—Booth had broken his leg.

We stopped at a house out in the Maryland countryside and I looked out into an adjoining field and said that (psychically) I saw two riders approaching on horses, and that one waited in the field while the other seemed to rush toward the door of the house. There was an aura of anxiety and urgency to their visit. The docent confirmed that my vision was correct.

John Wilkes Booth had hooked up with co-conspirator David Herold, who rode with him until they reached this countryside home.

I also perceived that there was either a doctor in residence at this house, or one that lived very nearby that could be summoned to this house. Again I was told that this was correct, that the house had been the home of Dr. Samuel Mudd.

Mudd and Booth had already met on at least two occasions In the previous six months. Mudd had even accepted an invitation from Booth to accompany him to his hotel room, where they had drinks and supposedly discussed horses and land. Now Booth was here to ask the doctor for help for his broken leg.

The doctor set Booth's leg and then allowed Booth to stay for close to twelve hours. While investigating the home and the room in which Booth had stayed, I discerned that the room had been changed somewhat, that the bed was originally in a different position, and that a new doorway had been cut into the room, or a doorway had been moved. I also saw that Booth was writing in a diary or journal of some sort, and again all of these visions were proven to be correct.

Throughout my investigation, protests were made that Booth had allegedly been in disguise and that Mudd wouldn't have recognized him, but my psychic senses told me otherwise. I'm not accusing Mudd of being a conspirator, but it's interesting to discover that Booth knew where to stop for help, and that Dr. Mudd, a man who had met Booth up close and personal at least twice and was face-to-face with him while tending his broken leg, wouldn't recognize him. I couldn't buy it then, and I can't buy it now. And when questioned by military authorities Dr. Mudd was able to give them an exact description of Booth; so how could he not have known it was the man with whom he had shared drinks?

Plus, Booth's notoriety would have made him recognizable to most people anyway. One historian told us that Booth was the Tom Cruise of his day.

A military commission found Dr. Mudd guilty of aiding and conspiring in a murder, and he was sentenced to life imprisonment, escaping the death penalty by a single vote. And despite repeated attempts by family members and others to have Dr. Mudd's record expunged, his conviction has never been overturned.

While investigating at the Mudd House we experienced, and managed to capture on film, some amazing paranormal phenomena.

I discerned the spirit of Mrs. Mudd, including her physical description which accurately matched a photograph of her in the house. While upstairs we all heard a loud snap coming from downstairs, like the sound of a stick or branch being broken in two.

"There's our ghost," I said, and we made our way downstairs.

I was also being filmed on a FLIR camera—forward-looking

infrared radiation—which captures thermal energy regardless of how much light is in a room, registering heat in white tones and cold in black tones. I believe that our pilot may have been the first to make use of FLIR in paranormal investigations.

As I stood downstairs I sensed a strong female presence off to my right, and I said aloud, "Mrs. Mudd?"

I asked her if she was the cause of the sound that we had all heard and she replied yes.

I said to everyone that she was walking toward me, and that I felt a tremendous coldness. "She's passing right through me," I said, "she's walking right through me."

As I said that the FLIR camera captured black footprints on the floor (black indicating cold) from shoes that appeared to be period-era shoes, and you can see the footprints approach me and then pass through me and continue on the other side. On the film you can clearly see that the ghostly footprints are woman-sized and shaped. No one else had recently walked in that same direction or in that area, and if it were a living being who had walked there the footprints would have registered as white, the FLIR having captured the heat of their emitted thermal energy. It was quite a dramatic moment.

Shortly after that manifestation we were regrouping to continue filming when one of the Mudd descendants came in from outside, rather shaken and breathless.

The sheriff's department sent regular patrols around the Mudd property. He had notified the department that a film crew would be there and that if they saw vehicles parked and lights on in the buildings, all was well.

He had also gone outside and secured all of the outbuildings, turning off all of the lights and locking all of the doors. One of those buildings was apparently a kitchen of sorts with running water.

After the spirit of Mrs. Mudd had walked through me he went outside to check on things during the break in filming and had found all of the doors to be unlocked, lights on, and water running.

Again I was asked if I felt that Booth had become repentant. And again, my answer was no.

Next they took me out in the middle of the toolies to a desolate median strip on Virginia Highway 301. There was no indication of the significance of the area. I had a vision of people creeping up with guns drawn and that was confirmed as correct. I was tuning in to the events of April 26, 1865 when the highway median strip was a working farm, owned by Richard Garrett. Booth and Herold were sleeping in the tobacco barn on Garrett's farm, not knowing that the 16th New York Cavalry had been tipped off as to the whereabouts of their hideout.

I sensed a powerful showdown about to occur which would lead to a climactic event.

The men surrounded the barn in the early morning hours and called for Booth and Herold to surrender. Herold decided to surrender. Booth dug in his heels and would not.

My visions revealed to me that Booth would meet his death on this very spot soon, a fact of which I was historically unaware. The men of the New York Cavalry set fire to the barn to flush Booth out, but he refused to surrender and as he was wobbling around in the barn on his broken leg a cavalryman, Sergeant Boston Corbett, who was watching Booth through the cracks in the barn and had trained his gun on Booth, fired, intending to wound Booth, but due to Booth's erratic manner of movement Corbett wound up shooting Booth in the neck.

I picked up on an extremely strong sensation of death, and the tour guide who was with us confirmed that Booth died within five yards of where I was standing.

To the very end, I perceived that Booth remained unrepentant.

Sadly, for all of the fine work that everyone put into the making of the TV pilot it never aired. I've never been told exactly why it was canned; I have some suspicions: we may have ruffled too many feathers along the way with my insights, and someone with clout may have protested effectively enough to shut the series down. I also became aware that there were jealous rivals attempting to sabotage my success with the show. For whatever reasons, it didn't air; and what a shame. I've only hit the high spots in writing about my experience. Jim, my producer, told me at the time of filming that we had gathered enough impressive material to make several episodes, not just one, and that he would be hard pressed to condense it down into a half-hour pilot episode. I saw the fine cut when it was finished, and he did a wonderful job. It accurately captured what I saw and experienced and shared during our investigation and was put together in a wonderfully entertaining way.

I can truthfully say that, of all the paranormal TV shows I've watched, I believe that ours would have been the leader of the pack.

When camera and crew, including the reenactors, went to the locations to film where we had performed my investigation, they reported encountering such phenomenon as objects visibly moving on their own and other interesting manifestations. I'd love to be able to go back and do it all over again.

Remember the way I was raised, and the fact that I'd carry grocery sacks to cars for ladies? I was too deferential and polite to the folks I encountered in my investigation, especially the women, as I had been raised to be.

Now I would be much more forceful in presenting my psychic insights.

CHAPTER **15**

Salem

MARJORIE AND I took a lot of road trips together, enjoying ourselves immensely. I would usually drive while she would indulge in one of her favorite pastimes: snoozing in the car as I drove, particularly if I had music playing either from the radio or from a CD. She always said it was some of the best sleep she ever had.

With me being a psychic and paranormal investigator, and with her sharing my intense interest in the paranormal, we decided a road trip to Salem, Massachusetts was not only a natural, but a must.

As with Lincoln's assassination I could feel the enormous energy still resident in the psychic atmosphere in Salem. You can't murder twenty innocent people for being "witches" and allow another five to die in jail without there being paranormal repercussions present for centuries to come.

While we did experience a few rather low-key phenomena, and of course my psychic senses were going wild, the most spectacular physical evidence that was shared by more than just Marjorie and myself was when we went with several others on a guided nighttime ghost walk.

Part of the walk included heading down the sidewalk by the Howard Street Cemetery which lies adjacent to the abandoned and very haunted Old Salem Jail. There's a wire fence for a distance of, best I remember, most of the way down the block that fences off the cemetery, and naturally you can see into the cemetery through the fence from top to bottom for the entire length that it stretches.

There are houses across the street from the cemetery, so our ghost walk guide gathered us all together and requested that we be respectfully quiet and talk in hushed tones; not because of the cemetery but out of respect for the people living in the houses across the street so as not to disturb them and earn complaints to the ghost walk company.

The guide then gave us a bit of the lore about the cemetery and the abandoned jail. Although electricity had been cut off to the jail for years electric lights could occasionally be seen inside it turning on and off, as well as other ghostly phenomena. Glowing orbs of light and other phantoms could be seen in the cemetery.

As is typical of any gathering of people, about a third of our group were openly mocking skeptics; about a third were believers; and about a third were just there to enjoy the tour, not really having an opinion or a belief one way or the other. Well, let me tell you: By the time the tour was over I don't believe there was a skeptic left among the bunch.

It was dark when we began our march down the sidewalk, and I really don't remember now but there either must have been a full moon, or close to it, and/or plenty of streetlights along the way because we could see fairly clearly into the cemetery for a good way and we could also see the hulk of the old, abandoned jail across the way. Even though it was dark you could see far enough into the cemetery to tell if someone was walking around in there with a flashlight trying to pull off a prank.

It was a warm evening, and as we continued our walk by the cemetery the air suddenly became absolutely chilly. It got so cold that several in our party could be heard whispering loudly about the change in temperature: "Wow. Do you feel that? It just suddenly got cold."

Then the noises began from within the cemetery, so close to the fence that you could tell that they were disembodied voices and sounds. People started freaking out. "Listen. Did you hear that? What was that?"

One particularly loud voice from within the cemetery blathered at Marjorie and me from a distance of only four or five feet away.

"Hush," she scolded me, thinking I had made the noise as a prank while she wasn't looking at me. "You're going to scare people."

"It wasn't me," I told her.

Then we began to see the shadow figures moving about in the cemetery, and the occasional glowing orb of light. Finally people began to see lights flickering in the old jail.

At the end of the sidewalk it turned, and we followed it up a busy street parallel to the backside of the cemetery and around to the old, abandoned jail, which stood looming ominously in the darkness.

We gathered together as a group and our guide began to speak to us. Suddenly Marjorie whipped around to face me and said sternly, "Don't do that in public."

"What?" I asked, bumfuzzled.

"Pinch my butt."

I began to laugh, for I had been standing about three or four feet away from her and I explained to her that I had not touched her.

A ghost had pinched her butt while we stood there in the gathering darkness.

I wonder if it was one of those old prisoners getting another jolly in after having been locked up for all of those years, or just a mischievous spirit who decided to help further enliven our tour.

Sadly—I've learned as I write this—the Old Salem Jail has now been turned into luxury apartments, a restaurant, and an exhibit space. Now *that's* haunting.

CHAPTER **16**

Cornwall/The Haunted Camera

WHILE LIVING IN Cornwall, Marjorie and I were nearly constantly bombarded by the paranormal. Some events you might consider insignificant but rest assured that any communication at all from the Other Side should be treated with respect and appreciation.

What do these manifestations mean? I think some are meant to give us guidance for our lives. Some, if followed, can be literally lifesaving. Others I believe to be "text messages" from the Other Side: "How ya doin'?" "How's your day?" "Hey, I'm here; just want you to know."

Others, I believe, come from spirits with a strong sense of humor. And/or objects that are either haunted to begin with or become haunted. Items such as our Haunted Camera.

In my lifetime I became both a professional fine artist (a painter) and a photographer. One day Marjorie and I were shopping at one of the large chain department stores and they had a small toy section and on one shelf was a toy camera, about the actual size of a regular 35mm camera body. It had a film advance button that made a noise; a shutter release button that made a shutter noise; a knob that when turned played different short musical pieces; and two LED lights in its built-in flash, one colored red and one colored green that would light up in an alternating sequence for a few seconds.

I started playing with it and it amused me so much that I began to laugh. "I have to have this," I told Marjorie, who responded by rolling her eyes. It was my gag gift to myself, and also a reminder to not take myself too seriously as an artist: After all, I imagine some folks buy a Picasso strictly for its investment value or because it matches a room's color scheme. Artists do take what we do seriously, yes, but…we're not curing cancer.

Turns out that buying that toy camera was beneficial to me—and to Marjorie, too—in more ways than one.

I put the camera in my office in our home and I would occasionally look at it and smile. Sometimes I'd play with it…a nod to my own childhood.

And then the little toy camera began to play back.

It started going off all by itself. Occasionally the music would play, but mostly it was the shutter noise. Just a few times, at first, with some long pauses in between. But then the little camera's "communications" became more frequent and the shutter noise more long-lasting.

I began to carry the camera around with me from room to room in our home, and its performance continued no matter its location.

Sometimes the shutter noises would be crisp and rapid fire. Other times they would be slow, almost drawn out, with pauses before the next one.

At first we took it as a sign that the Other Side was using the camera as a means of communication with us: "Hi. We're here." And we also entertained the thought that perhaps the camera itself was either "haunted" or somehow cognizant. Maybe it was sending us messages that it was happy that we had brought it into our home. And maybe all of the above were true.

But then we began to notice that the camera's greatest periods of activity were prescient. They always indicated some type of change which was about to occur in our lives. Sometimes those changes were small; other times they were of great significance.

The camera always seemed to anticipate when we were about to decide to take a road trip, for example, noisily clicking away in rapid-fire succession.

At first the camera only went off during the day, but then it became active during the night too. We would talk to it (or the spirit or spirits behind its activation) and tell them we appreciated their communication and to have a good night. Sometimes that would quiet the camera down; other times it would send it into a flurry of response.

One of the camera's particularly active periods turned out to be a prediction of my return to radio.

I had done a few radio interviews back in 1998 and 2000, and then in 2001 in response to the 9-11 terrorist attacks.

But beginning in 2003, shortly after the camera had been going nuts for days on end, my radio appearances increased dramatically, rather suddenly, and nearly all at once. The invitations began to pour in out of the blue and thereafter I was a featured guest on several radio shows—including regular appearances on some large popular stations whose DJs were almost celebrities themselves—on stations in New York, Wisconsin, Missouri, Texas, and Arkansas.

Altogether my run on radio lasted fourteen years.

Radio appearances where I was an ongoing featured guest were typically for an hour's duration, live, during which I gave short, free readings of about thirty seconds to two minutes on the air, as well as answered questions about the paranormal and spiritual matters, performed dream interpretations, etc.

At two different points in time I was a regular featured guest on four different radio stations each month, with monthly appearances lasting several consecutive years on each station, and on one of those stations I appeared weekly during that timeframe.

According to the feedback from the DJs, on nearly every single station on which I was appearing I jammed the phone lines each and every appearance, with the listener phone calls beginning before I was even on the air and sometimes lasting for several hours afterward as callers tried to reach me.

On the air at one station I regularly blew up their phone lines so badly that not only could listeners not reach the station, but the station's employees also couldn't manage to make an outside call for a short period of time.

And at one radio station several listeners that had some of the DJs personal cell phone numbers would begin calling those numbers in an attempt to talk to me.

I enjoyed those years immensely, and then suddenly it all came crashing down in sequence, through no fault or desire of my own.

But that's a story that continues a few years down the road, when we left New York for Florida.

The haunted toy camera continued to chatter away for years on end, nearly always presaging some interesting turn of events in our lives.

Guidance and communication can come to us in many different forms if we will be receptive.

CHAPTER **17**

A Knock in the Attic

ONE OF THE most dramatic manifestations that occurred in our beautiful New York home was a loud knock from the attic.

It started shortly after I moved from Texas to be with Marjorie. She had bought a house in upstate New York. It was two stories, with a basement and an attic. The house had been built almost 200 years ago by the time I came to live with Marjorie, and in some respects the old house had better construction than some modern homes. I fell in love with it as soon as I saw it, but the cherry on the frosting was the fact that a shallow, clear, beautiful stream flowed right by our house, not thirty feet away.

I spent many happy hours sitting outside by that stream, just watching and listening to the water as it flowed. I also loved to photograph the stream during the changing seasons.

Shortly after moving in I inspected the house inside and out from top to bottom, attic to basement. I upgraded door and window locks and we reset the passcode for the alarm system. Our home was secure.

So one day we were both astonished to hear this loud, repeated knocking coming from the attic.

Now, the house was secure, as I said. The alarm had a feature so that even when it was deactivated a chime would go off if any of the doors were opened. We kept all doors and windows closed and locked, plus I worked from home, providing readings for my growing clientele, and guesting on various radio shows. In other

115

words it would be awfully hard for an intruder to sneak into our home.

Plus the entrance to the attic was on the second floor of our home, through our bathroom. There was a door, almost full-sized like a regular door, that opened to a stairwell that led up into the space above. So again, it would be virtually impossible for anyone to sneak into the house and find their way up there. And why would an intruder enter our home in order to make the loft their destination anyway?

Nonetheless I climbed the stairs to the second floor, opened the locked door in our bathroom, turned the attic lights on, climbed those stairs and stood looking around the mostly empty space. The attic was large, and the ceiling was tall. The only things stored there were a large wardrobe with its door flung wide open, a few scattered boxes, and a small pile of lumber against one wall.

There was one window and I checked to make sure that it was securely closed and locked and not banging in the wind.

Of course no one was there in a physical body. I felt a slight chill and I spoke aloud, asking any spirits who might be present to make themselves known. I let them know that we had heard them, and I asked them if they had any particular message for either of us. I waited a bit and receiving nothing I shrugged, bade them welcome, and went back down the stairs into the house.

From that point onward, and over the span of several years, the knocking intensified both in volume and frequency.

And when I say intensified, I mean intensified. What started as a kind of muffled *thump-thump-thump* increased to a *bang-bang-bang* that sounded as if someone were attacking a rafter with a hammer to a *thwack-thwack-thwack* that sounded as if someone were attacking the house with a large sledgehammer.

I heard it. Marjorie heard it. Her son Eric heard it. Our cats heard it and would become bushy-tailed and wild-eyed, running and finding hiding places for awhile.

I had inspected the attic and knew nothing was amiss there, and that there was nothing physical that could be causing the noise.

I walked the entire perimeter of the house, visually inspecting every square foot of our home carefully, especially the side of the house where the window to the attic was located, searching for any loose flashing, anything that could account for the noise. The house was in excellent shape. Plus, occasionally when I was outside, such as one time when I was inspecting that side of the house where the attic's window was located, I could hear the banging in the attic from outside. There was no wind blowing, nothing flapping in the breeze outside. Just the sound of the supernatural noise emanating from our home.

We all got used to it; except for the cats, who would all run and hide when it started. The knocking didn't seem to have any rhyme or reason and would happen during the day as well as at night. Fortunately for our sleep patterns, it happened much more frequently during the day, and if it happened at night it was slightly muffled, as if in consideration of the hour.

Unbeknownst to us the knocking had become so loud that the neighbors could now hear it when they were out in their yards; and sometimes while in their houses. I found that out quite by accident when I walked across the street to this delightful restaurant that faced our home. I was sitting at the bar enjoying a drink when our neighbor came in and as we struck up a conversation she eventually inquired about the loud banging and knocking coming from our home.

"Oh. Uh...we're having some remodeling done," I lied, trying to think quick on my feet. This particular neighbor was not privy to my psychic goings-on.

"So late in the evening?"

"Well, sometimes that's the only time we can coordinate for our guy to come."

"Oh," she said, seeming unconvinced as she shrugged her shoulders and walked away.

I hadn't realized the power of the enthusiasm our guys in the attic had for communicating their presence. Now, occasionally, the neighbors would also be besieged by their noise.

Sometimes there would be a few knocks and then silence the rest of the day. At other times, the knocking would happen two or three times a day, at irregular intervals. Then there would be the prolonged series of knocks that would last for a good minute or so. It did indeed sound like someone doing demo or remodeling.

And then, just when we thought that the knocking had gotten as loud and obtrusive as it possibly could, the spirits managed to ramp up the decibels even more. That lured me back into the attic, where I discovered that the pile of lumber had been moved away from the wall, and there, on the attic floor—presumably having been covered by the lumber for all of this time—was a small heart cut from lace fabric, measuring about two inches tall by two and a half inches wide.

I knelt down, picked it up and scooted the lumber back into place. I didn't receive any particular message or communication from the spirit or spirits who had given me this revelation, so I thanked them for their gift and took it downstairs with me to show to Marjorie.

After that...the knocking stopped entirely and never occurred again. We actually kind of missed hearing it. But the cats didn't.

I took the lace heart and put it with the chunk of wood I had found in my bowl of chili. I have them both to this day.

And the next time I ran into that neighbor she said, "So, finally got your remodeling done, have you? I haven't heard anymore banging coming from your house."

CHAPTER **18**

Uri Geller

WHEN I WAS a young man living in San Angelo, Texas in the 1970s a controversial figure burst onto the scene. Uri Geller, an Israeli-born psychic, had become prominent in Europe and then the U.S.

My mother and I were reading everything we could get our hands on that offered any information about the paranormal: *Psychic Discoveries Behind the Iron Curtain; Seth Speaks;* and of course Uri's *My Story.*

I was hungry for religious and spiritual truth; even as a boy of twelve I had learned that there was a lot of hokum in both the mainline religious and occult belief systems. So from that age forward I studied and I read. Some things rang true; others didn't. Someone who did ring true was Uri, and as the years went by I was astonished at the criticism and ridicule that came to be heaped upon him.

Uri became a person I looked up to, someone with whom I could identify. And I was amazed at his celebrity and his growing wealth.

See, my family was poor. Living on mostly borrowed money we were able to maintain a precarious façade of stability, but it was mostly bank loans, a succession of ratty old used cars without the air-conditioning that would have saved us from the fierce West Texas heat—and a deteriorating house that no one had the resources to repair.

My family mismanaged what money they had, never learned sound economics, and unfortunately passed that ignorance on to me.

The family mindset was that some people were born lucky and got all the breaks, and others didn't. We were one of those that didn't. "People like us aren't meant to have money. It's just the way things are," was the refrain I heard repeated frequently in my childhood home.

So to see Uri, someone else who had a gift like mine, rise up to fame and fortune impressed me greatly. At the time I would have emulated him if I could, but I was crippled by my family's lack of knowledge about sound financial practices and our negative belief system.

I watched Uri's TV appearances and followed the print news about him over the years, never once conceiving of the possibility that one day I would actually meet Uri face-to-face.

After I had moved to New York and was living with Marjorie, for some reason that I can't even recall now, I began corresponding with…Uri Geller. We exchanged not only e-mails but "snail mail:" actual physical correspondence as well. These exchanges weren't starstruck fan mails from me to him; we carried on extremely specific and detailed discussions regarding various aspects of the paranormal, among other minor issues.

Worth mentioning is the fact that at the time I did not have a photograph of myself on my psychic website, nor did I share one with Uri either through e-mails or regular mail. Had he passed by me on the street he wouldn't have had a clue—from my physical appearance—as to who I was.

One day I discovered news that Uri would be appearing in person in Manhattan to hold a lecture and demonstration. We purchased tickets and went to see him. Marjorie had asked me before if I felt he was the real deal, and I had always replied in the affirmative. "But," I told her as we made the drive into Manhattan, "I'll know beyond a shadow of a doubt when I see him in person, and if I can somehow lay my hands on him, if I can somehow just touch him, even for a brief moment, my gift will tell me everything I need to know."

We took our seats in the venue and I excused myself to use the restroom. As I was walking toward the restroom the door opened and who do you think came out? Uri. My opportunity had been granted to me. He smiled at me and I smiled at him and as he walked by me I reached out my hand and gave him a couple of friendly pats on his shoulder. And my psychic senses confirmed, through that exploratory touch, that Uri was, as I had always maintained, the genuine article.

I returned to my seat and Uri began his lecture and demonstration. Even though I knew beyond a shadow of a doubt that Uri was the real deal I kept my eye peeled for trickery. I had been an avid fan of magic since I was a kid—David Copperfield was another of my heroes—and I watched Uri like a hawk for any evidence of chicanery. I could not discern any legerdemain.

And then came the famous spoon bending demonstration. I had read about Uri's "violent" manipulations of spoons which would cause them to bend or ultimately break. I had read that Uri used special faked or gimmicked spoons. That night Uri dumped a selection of spoons out onto a table and invited someone to come up and pick one, and to examine it. We all watched closely as a person chose one, examined it closely and carefully, and tried to bend it by force and could not. I watched as the person handed that spoon to Uri, who used enough force himself to indicate that it was a strong, sturdy, regular spoon that would be difficult to bend using the force of your arms and hands, and then he banged it loudly on the table several times. When he proceeded with his demonstration I was astonished at how different his in-person performance was from how his critics usually described it, for Uri held the spoon very lightly at the very tip end of the handle and stroked the area of the spoon near the bowl with the lightest feather of a touch, the spoon not even bowing downward under the slight pressure of his finger.

As he stroked the spoon lightly it began to bend, evoking gasps of surprise and awe from the audience. At one point he removed his finger from the spoon entirely, merely making stroking motions through

A Knock in the Attic

the air above the spoon and the spoon continued to bend. It was a most convincing and believable exhibition.

What made the evening even more delightful was when, in an almost spontaneous outburst of enthusiasm, several audience members suddenly pulled their own spoons out that they themselves had bent psychically and showed them to Uri.

I had experimented with, and had been successful, with telekinesis myself, and I knew that others were also capable of such feats, not just the world-famous Geller.

Man, who would have thought that I—the raised-in-poverty young kid from an overgrown cow town—would not only correspond with but would see in person one of my idols from youth. But the evening would get even better.

Uri was signing books after his demonstration, and we got in line for him to sign my copy.

When it was my turn Uri took my book, opened it, looked up at me and smiled, and then hesitated a moment.

"Wait a minute," he said. "We know each other."

I smiled and nodded.

Uri continued. "We've corresponded. Both via e-mails and regular mails, too." Again I nodded affirmation. "This is our first meeting face-to-face, though. Before now everything has been through correspondence. And we didn't discuss trivial matters; our letters have been extremely detailed and concerned specific subjects. And we've exchanged several e-mails and letters."

I again agreed that he was correct, introduced myself, we shook hands, and Uri signed my book, while onlookers that had heard our exchange stood by in awe.

Wow. Just…wow. When I was in my youth, living in that old house in West Texas, I never would have thought that this experience would come to be a treasured part of my life in the future.

But the story's not over yet.

This book is actually a prequel to one that I published in September of 2020. That book, titled *Riding with Ghosts, Angels, and the Spirits of the Dead*, deals with a short span of time in my life but one that is paranormally meaningful. Professionals in the writing industry as well as readers have said that the book is unique, that there is nothing else out there like it. It's a collection of true ghost stories, encounters that I experienced while riding my motorcycle thousands of miles. But more than just a collection of ghost stories, each unique essay—in addition to being entertaining to read—offers up a spiritual truth or insight for further contemplation: insights such as the fact that powerful, unseen intelligences on the Other Side observe us and listen to us; communicate with us in astonishing ways; are sometimes able to grant our desires; may offer us further insights into the spiritual realm; and can literally save our lives…if we'll listen to them and pay attention.

Everything I read said that an author needs to get celebrity endorsements for their books. I approached several celebrities, without success, and started to rack my brain as to who I could approach that might give me their favorable review of my book.

A light bulb went off: Uri Geller.

It had been years since I had corresponded with him. I no longer had his e-mail address as the mail account I had used in those years had been closed and through my moves over the years I had lost track of many e-mail addresses.

I went to his website and used the contact e-mail address given there, hoping against hope. I included a PDF file of my book, asked Uri for his endorsement, and reminded him that we used to correspond and of our meeting at his demonstration, hoping that he would remember me. I sent the e-mail and tried to put my hopes out of my mind and get on about the day's business.

Later that day when I checked my e-mail there was a response from Uri. The same day, mind you. And he graciously wrote this about my book: "John Russell's *Riding with Ghosts, Angels, and the Spirits of the Dead* is an incredible supernatural journey that will mesmerize your soul." — Uri Geller.

I was overwhelmed with gratitude and replied to tell him so and to thank him for his gracious and quick response.

Thank you again, Uri. I count you as my friend.

And also, once again, Uri is the real deal.

And if you don't believe me, just ask the CIA.

CHAPTER **19**

Signs

MANY SIGNS CONTINUED to manifest in our Cornwall home. It was abundantly evident that beings on the Other Side were close to us, making themselves known. As I've said before, some of those communications or protections have been life-saving, as with the seventeen major gas leaks in my old home. At other times I'm convinced that those on the Other Side of this life are just saying Hi, letting us know that they're there, watching over us, or perhaps just seeking companionship or a simple connection with someone else, much in the same manner that we strike up brief small talk conversations with strangers in the grocery store, at the bus stop, and so on. And then sometimes there are communications that may not be life-saving but are most assuredly helpful. Such as the running-water sound.

I had set up our Cornwall basement as a multipurpose space: In one area I stored my gardening tools; in another section I placed my mechanic's tools; one space was devoted to my artistic painting, including a place for my paints, brushes, painting knives, and so on; and in yet another part of the basement was the most important and sacred zone of all, a circle I had psychically and magically inscribed in a nearly perfectly square area of the cellar and in which I performed my prayers, rituals, and meditations, and frequently received guidance and communications from the other side, as well as some amazing manifestations.

Imagine, if you will, a circle drawn inside of a square, but the circle doesn't touch or even come close to the borders of the square. My invisible circle left a border of a few feet all the way around it, so it did not touch the square portion in which it was located. That description will be extremely significant in a story to come.

I was often up and down the stairs in our home, from my office on the second floor to the first floor of our home and down into the basement and back up again. When I had some breaks between clients it would not be uncommon for me to run down to the basement for something and then go back upstairs.

On my scheduled days off I would spend hours in the basement, painting, meditating, sorting my tools, etc.

One day while moving about the house I heard the distinct sound of water running through pipes. I was there alone, and I knew that I had not left any faucets open with water running. Fearing a water leak, my first thought was to check the outside faucets. Those all proved to be turned off and none were leaking.

Next I walked through the house, checking every faucet there was. All were turned off, and none were leaking.

I went down to the basement where the sound of running water became louder. I looked around and could not find any source for the noise. I was stymied. I stood there for a moment, and then it hit me: I wasn't hearing physical water running through the pipes, I was hearing a paranormal manifestation. But to what purpose?

"Guys," I said, "what are you trying to tell me? I don't get it."

The sound of the running water intensified.

"Guys, I'm sorry, but I don't understand. And I have to go back upstairs to my office now, because I have a client shortly. Make it clear to me whatever it is you're trying to communicate, please."

Nothing.

So I returned to my office, provided my client with their reading, and then headed back down to the basement where the sound of running water seemed to be the loudest.

"Okay, guys, I'm back. Now what's going on?"

I stood still and became quiet and receptive. Our washer and dryer were in the basement, and I had the sudden inspiration to inspect the washer. For some odd reason, the drain hose on our washing machine wasn't one piece. A section of the hose came from the drain on the washing machine and attached to one end of a connector. From that connecter another section of hose led to the drain into which the water from the washing machine pumped to enter into the sewer lines.

I had just recently used the washing machine and everything had worked fine, but somehow the lower section of hose had detached itself from the connector, and if I hadn't noticed that, then the next time I did laundry the machine would have emptied its water directly into the basement, making a minor flooding mess and possibly creating an electrical hazard and danger to boot. You see, the electrical outlet for the machines sat directly above the washer and if the pressure of the draining water caused the hose to flail about it could have sprayed water directly into that electrical outlet.

Seeing the problem I said, "Oh, wow guys; thanks."

And with that the sound of water running through the pipes immediately ceased.

When the stream that was so close to our house would periodically become swollen from rains or snowmelt, the water table would rise so high that water would seep up through the ground and through the concrete of our basement, and even though we had a sump pump the water would occasionally overpower the pump's ability to discharge it and we would find an inch or more of water covering the entire basement floor.

I would go down and try to keep the little pump running while I also vacuumed up water with my shop vacuum.

One time we had a minor flooding incident and water had covered the basement floor to a depth of about one half inch, but the pump handled it admirably and soon there was just a wet sheen remaining over the basement floor, but still wet enough that you'd leave discernible footprints when you walked through it.

Marjorie came halfway down the basement stairs to look at the result and while we were talking she asked if I had noticed anything strange. I remarked that I hadn't, and she laughed like she couldn't believe what I'd said.

"Look at your ritual circle," she said, pointing to that section of the basement.

I looked, and water had surrounded the circular ritual space; but inside my circle it was completely bone dry. Every other square inch of the basement floor was wet, but when I walked to my ritual circle space and bent down to touch my hand to the floor, it was bone dry.

Water had covered every single bit of the basement floor to a depth of a half inch or so…except for that highly charged space in which I performed rituals, meditated, prayed, and received strong communications from the Other Side.

It was a powerful visual reminder that psychic and supernatural forces are not only real, but that they can impact the physical realm in dramatic ways.

There were other interesting paranormal manifestations involving water. I mentioned that I loved to photograph the beautiful stream that ran by our home.

At the time I was shooting film, not digital, and I would eagerly await the development of my photographs from the lab up the street.

I opened the envelope containing my photos and as I looked at them I was astonished to see the clear visage of a woman in the stream. Her appearance was all in white, and you can clearly discern her closed eyes, eyebrows, hair, nostrils, lips, and even part of her torso. Her mouth is open as if she might be singing or saying something. Everyone who has seen the photograph has been amazed.

I showed it to my photography instructor, and she asked me if I had Photoshopped the image, that's how incredible it was. I assured her that I had not, and I told her, in truth, that at the time I didn't even know how to use Photoshop.

Another developed print came back to me revealing the image of a jack-o'-lantern grinning up at me from under the water of the stream. The body of the jack-o'-lantern is an orange pumpkin and is clearly visible as the color orange in the photograph; as well, it sports a green stem, and the typical carved face. It's a wonderfully bizarre image.

Oddities involving my phone frequently occurred.

I received an interesting message on my answering machine one day. A woman told me in the message that she had been at work and had seen a ghost. After seeing the ghost she heard a voice tell her to "Call John Russell." Subsequently, she explained, she looked me up on the Internet and called to leave me this message, including her phone number.

I called that number many times but never got an answer, and there was never an answering machine or voice mail that picked up. It would just ring and ring until I finally gave up and hung up the phone.

And I had several clients tell me that during our phone readings they would sometimes hear strange noises in their homes, feel touches on their bodies, or both.

The realm of spirit seems to be fairly adroit at manipulating or utilizing phones, something that was really demonstrated to me in a couple of amazing ways in stories that I write about in *Riding with Ghosts, Angels, and the Spirits of the Dead.*

Late one evening I went shopping at our nearest Walmart store.

I had entered a hardware section of the store and on the top shelf in one section was a large display of chrome trailer hitch balls. The balls were encased in sturdy cardboard boxes with open fronts so that you could see the ball, and the whole box was wrapped in clear plastic. I had paused momentarily to look at something, and I looked up to see one of the boxes begin to move slowly forward on the shelf. As I watched, the box continued to move slowly and steadily toward the edge of the shelf. When it was about to topple off I hurried over and caught it just as it fell.

Spirits follow me everywhere, and frequently make me aware of their presence by just such astonishing means of communication.

CHAPTER **20**

A Very Unstable Stable

I WAS FREQUENTLY asked to conduct paranormal investigations, such as the investigation of a haunted horse barn across the New York state border to which I was asked to travel in order to conduct an investigation of events that were spooking stable hands and horses alike.

I was asked by the groom if I could come and shed some light on the many experiences they were having. And, they wanted to know, were they or the horses in any kind of danger? During my three hour investigation I was able to provide comfort to those involved, hopefully including the horses; I discerned many facts associated with the area that the stable hands were able to confirm; and there was a good amount of confirming paranormal phenomena: they weren't just imagining things.

Altogether there was a handful of us at the stable, and folks were mighty interested to see how this would all play out as I began my investigation.

I began by getting to know the parties involved and by asking them to tell me some of their experiences.

I was regaled with amazing stories that the groom and others had experienced: horses' feed buckets by their stalls would lift up by themselves and then loudly flop back down against the posts on which they were hung.

Supernatural winds would blow through the horse barn from one end to the other, even when it was completely still outside of the barn with no wind at all—not even a slight breeze.

A radio that was kept in the barn would turn on and off by itself, and its volume would raise and lower, also independent of human hands.

The sound of someone loudly whistling a tune would occasionally be heard.

As we were discussing these experiences I asked the groom, "Did you once get so flabbergasted by the manifestations that you just up and ran out of the barn to escape the intensity, running so fast and so blindly that you nearly ran into something?"

They laughed and confirmed that my vision was correct.

I had tuned into the situation and the first thing I was able to assure them of was the fact that no one there was in any danger, including the horses. I explained that the spirits were active, yes, but not malevolent.

Why were the spirits so active there? they wanted to know.

That's always the sixty-four thousand dollar question.

When we're dealing with the Other Side, we're dealing with a mostly invisible unknown: Who is there, and what do they want? What are they trying to communicate? Is this some kind of spectral "recording" that is left behind in the atmosphere that replays over and over, or are there sentient beings from the realm of spirit involved? Are these the souls or spirits of those who were once living in the flesh in this area, or angels or nature spirits or…

As you can see it's a complex issue to discern, and perfect and complete answers are often not forthcoming. We do the best we can.

It was nearing twilight as I began my investigation and the first thing I wanted to do was to walk the property, walk through the barn, get a general sense of things, and meet some of the horses who were out of their stalls and running free in the enclosed pasture.

The day had been calm with no wind, and indeed right now there was not so much as the slightest of breezes blowing. It was dead still outside. Nevertheless as we walked through the barn this stiff wind began behind us, blowing its way through the barn from one end to the other, stirring up dust and bits of debris as it blew, and when it reached me it was so strong that it nearly blew the cap off of my head, and again, it's important to note that when this phenomenon occurred there was not a leaf stirring on any tree outside. The ghostly wind was confined to the interior of the barn.

"That's what I was telling you about," the groom said.

We walked outside and they called the horses up to a section of the fence bordering the pasture and the stable.

Such beautiful animals. They allowed me to pet them and I decided to see if I could psychically communicate with them. To my surprise I could, and one horse in particular told me that it was none too happy with the manifestations inside the barn. I correctly identified that horse as the one which seemed to be the most spooked by the occurrences and had experienced the most supernatural events.

I talked to the horses both physically and psychically and explained to them what was going on, and that while it could be startling, they were in no danger and that no harm would come to them.

That seemed to placate them somewhat, and we continued the investigation.

During the evening I received many names which they were able to confirm as people who were definitely historically connected to either the area or to the horse barn itself.

I accurately discerned that there were many bodies buried in the immediate area, not only peoples' bodies but animals too, including horses.

As it got darker I asked them to extinguish most of the lights in the stable. I had brought a small flashlight with me and I wanted to walk through the stable several times in the semi-darkness and see if the night brought out any more manifestations. It did.

At one point I stopped and looked up at the rafters, stating that I felt someone had been hung in that spot. They told me that I had stopped in the exact location where the hanging was rumored to have occurred.

As the night wore on the groom closed both large doors to the stable, and in spite of the stable being closed up tightly yet once again the strong wind blew from one end of the stable to the other.

During the investigation, the radio would turn on and off by itself, and the volume would go up or down or sometimes shut off completely, and this occurred when we knew there was not anyone near the device, and sometimes it happened while we were watching it.

And we all heard, in the darkness while we were all grouped together, the loud whistling. I immediately flashed a light in the direction from which the sound had come and there was not a soul in the flesh to be seen.

As we were walking through a darkened portion of the barn a large glass door attached to a bulletin board type frame swung open and hit one of our party.

As I looked at the groom I watched their face change before my eyes, and when I told them the description of what I was seeing they informed me that I was accurately describing one of their grandparents.

And not surprisingly (as Native Americans lived everywhere on this continent) I picked up many Indian spirits, including one old Indian who had apparently cursed the area in retribution for some slight.

I said a prayer for him and asked him if he could persuade the Powers That Be to at least take it easy on the horses, and I also asked him if he could find some forgiveness in his heart for what had happened to him when he was in the flesh in this area of the state.

All in all it was a dynamic and dramatic paranormal investigation, teeming with marvelous manifestations of otherworldly power.

I was able to reassure the stable hands that while the events were indeed startling for the average person to experience that neither they nor the horses were in any danger, that they should remain calm and even address the spirits aloud and ask them if they could mitigate their demonstrations.

I explained that some of the events could be due to residual energy left in the atmosphere by such traumatic events as the hanging, and that they could smudge the barn to try and alleviate some of that imprinted negative energy.

Other happenings, I reasoned, could be just those "Hey, I'm here. Pay attention to me." types of occurrences that could be placated by acknowledging the spirits' presences and be further tamed by leaving small offerings of various kinds: small portions of food; candies; even a small glass of alcohol such as whiskey or gin (Some spirits seem to have a tremendous fondness for gin.).

The groom and others thanked me, and I left the area with a blessing and a prayer for all involved.

As the stable was some distance away for me to travel, and I had other pressing issues to deal with at the time, I never did an in-depth follow-up, but it remains one of the more exciting investigations I have done.

CHAPTER **21**

Florida

WE DECIDED TO move to Florida. We were both tired of shoveling snow all winter long, and where we lived upstate it was not uncommon to have two feet of the white stuff dumped on us one week, and another two feet the next. I remember once the outside thermometer registered 15 degrees below zero, and the high for the day was zero. That went on for nearly two weeks. We watched icicles hanging from our roof and neighbors' roofs grow to three feet or more in length.

And once the snow began to fall it didn't melt until late in the spring; sometimes it would be May and there would still be patches of snow on the ground here and there. Once the snow started to fall and the ground was covered in white it remained that way for four to six months. That wreaked havoc on my gardening.

So we bade farewell to our beloved home and stream and made our move. I miss that old home to this day.

We rented a house until our new Florida home could be built. We beat the movers down, so in the rental house we had a bed, some folding lawn chairs, and a radio. The kitchen had a refrigerator and a stove, and we ate out whenever we desired. It was pretty sparse digs until our furniture arrived, and we had no TV and I'm a TV junkie.

We had brought our three cats with us: Olivia, Zoe, and Sophie.

One evening we were all gathered in the den, we in our lawn chairs and the cats lying on the floor close by, listening to the radio and debating when we would go to bed. Suddenly all of us heard the sound of a key being inserted into the front door's lock. We heard the sound of the knob turning and the door opening and looked at each other in mild shock: who would have a key to this house but us? Would the landlord come over late in the evening and just let himself in without ringing the doorbell? Surely not.

The cats were all bug-eyed, tails bushing as they jumped up and ran to look into the living room, into which the front door opened.

By the time we moved to Florida I had recovered a great deal healthwise, so I sprang up out of my chair to go and confront this audacious and impudent intruder. As I headed toward the living room we all heard the loud sound of footsteps on the tiled area around the front door, and the noise of the front door closing. By then I had a clear view into the living room and the front door, where I saw...no one.

Nevertheless I searched that house inside and out and upside down, and of course there was no one present in a physical body anywhere.

Marjorie and I looked at each other, grinned and said, "Welcome to Florida."

The spirits were giving us a grand old welcome indeed.

In the room I chose for my office in our rental house I noticed a powerfully sweet aroma, like an expensive perfume, another sign that we were being welcomed to our new home state. When our new home was built and I moved into my office there, that exact same aroma manifested as well, which I took to be an extraordinarily good omen. And indeed, Florida has been good to us in many ways.

But back to the rental house.

We had brought the Haunted Camera along with us, and it began to click away noisily with its shutter noises and would also periodically play music.

It was so loud and raucous sometimes; one time it began to go off non-stop for a period of time while I was on the air with one of the radio stations on which I regularly appeared. The DJs all heard it and asked me what in the world was causing the racket, and I explained to them the story of the Haunted Camera. From then on it came to be a fixture on certain radio shows, happily clicking away in the background while I was on the air live.

But one of its wildest manifestations occurred one night when I had gone to bed. I placed the camera, turned to face our bed, on the long credenza that doubled as our TV stand. The little camera would periodically go off, the little red and green LEDs alternating as they flashed back and forth in sequence.

Suddenly the camera went off loudly in rapid-fire succession and from the area of the camera in which the LEDs are located a bright white light flashed, bright enough to light up the bedroom for a second, just as if the camera actually had a real built-in flash.

I could only tell Marjorie about it for she was in another area of the house at the time. The little camera has never done that since.

And I believe I know why, for it was one of the most important—to me, anyway—indicators of things to come.

I have been a biker since around the age of 15. I craved the pleasure of riding again, but I had been so sickly and so gimped up for so long that it was foolish to have a motorcycle wasting away in the garage.

But now my health had returned somewhat, and I was enjoying an astonishing degree of wellness, mobility, and strength.

I was watching the TV one night and a commercial for Honda motorcycles came on. Tax, title, license, and nothing down and I could be riding the bike of my dreams for $60 a month. I visited the dealership the next day and met Melissa. I know that's her name because that's what she told me. It was love at first sight, and man…I began to tear up the roads all over Florida and into the state of Georgia as well.

It was not uncommon for me to ride 1,500 to 1,800 miles a month, and that's while I was appearing on radio several times a month and I was also the busiest I had ever been reading for clients worldwide.

And with that awesome freedom to be able to roam afresh, I could also travel to and hike miles and miles through the gorgeous state parks, indulging once again my love for the woods and the outdoors. An average day might see me riding anywhere from 200 to 300 miles, visiting three or more state parks, and hiking a total of seven or eight miles. I was ecstatic.

You can read more about those adventures in my book, *Riding with Ghosts, Angels, and the Spirits of the Dead*.

Our New Home

I would park Melissa at one of our beautiful state parks and hike the trails. If there were benches anywhere in the parks I would sit for hours at a time, communing with nature and with nature spirits.

And Native American Indian spirits would also communicate with me. It was during one of these times that they informed me that hundreds of years ago, before there was any such thing as the technologies we have nowadays, that they would see UFOs flying through the skies. That effectively eliminates any arguments about whether or not these sightings are of man-made craft, for these sightings occurred for the Indians before any such technology as we have today existed.

Some Indian spirits also communicated to me that certain of their tribe had not only communicated with but had actually experienced contact with these space visitors, but the spirits seemed reticent to give me too many details, as if it might give away some sacred secret that was better kept intact for a while longer.

One native spirit that appeared to me as a youth asked if he could follow me home and just hang out awhile, enjoying our home and our company. I discerned no malevolence about the boy, and I said sure.

He had a good sense of humor and created a little harmless mischief in our home: He would vigorously rattle the door in our hallway that led into our laundry room. Once when we had been out and were coming into our house I unlocked that door and started to pull it open when the doorknob was forcibly grabbed from the other side and the door was pulled shut with a slight bang. I laughed and told him I appreciated that he was welcoming us home, and I thanked him for watching over our house, and by extension, us as well.

Sometimes he would engage me in a mild tug-of-war with that doorknob, which always got a laugh out of me.

He hung around for some years and then appeared to move on. We've had no more episodes with that door since.

A very odd thing happened when we moved into our new home: The Haunted Camera stopped making noise. I always kept fresh batteries in it so it could communicate with us, and I would periodically check it manually to make sure everything was still in working order, and it was. But when we built our new home and moved in, the little camera grew quiet and never gave another peep.

I guess we had arrived where we were supposed to be, at least for a while, and the little camera had said all it had to say.

As I mentioned I have been a popular radio and podcast guest. But sometime around the year 2011 that would all come to an end through no choice of my own. Radio stations began to change formats and focus. Suddenly it was no longer popular to have a regular psychic on the air each week or each month.

The DJs at one large, popular station told me that the station had been sold, the new owners had changed the format virtually overnight, and had cleaned house, firing everyone from top to bottom including the on-air talent, issuing the statement that everyone could reapply for their old job but there was no guarantee they'd be rehired.

But the most dramatic example given me was when the host of one station called me to inform me that we would not be doing radio anymore. When I inquired as to the reason, he told me that while he was live on the air new owners came in with armed guards, shut the station down, ordered all of the employees to gather their belongings in boxes and take them to their cars (while the armed guards watched) and then the building was emptied of everyone and they put a chain on the entrance doors to the station and padlocked the chain. "While I was live on the air, John; while I was live on the air."

My nine consecutive years of radio appearances were suddenly at an end. Damn it. I missed the on-air talents, and I missed my faithful callers. It left a large void in my life that nothing else could replace. That connection with others; there's nothing else quite like it.

I did have a couple of notable paranormal experiences on my motorcycle that I didn't include in *Riding with Ghosts*...

I was on a back country road that's straight and flat—as most Florida roads are—and this road was straight for miles and miles. And in a fairly common scenario there was no traffic on the road, either behind me or oncoming. I always check my rearview mirrors frequently and on this particular day there hadn't been anyone behind me since I'd turned onto the road.

I was approaching a highway intersection that's also straight and flat for miles and miles and I had just checked behind me and there was no one there. I continued to check my rearview mirrors as I slowed to stop for the sign at the intersection, and I'm all alone on the road. I stopped at the stop sign and out of nowhere this car was suddenly right behind me.

It startled me, because I knew I didn't have anyone behind me and there were no hidden driveways or dirt roads or anything where someone could have suddenly darted out without my having seen them. And for me it was unnerving to have looked in my rearview mirrors a second ago and then a second later glimpsing a car sitting on my tail.

I always double-check and sometimes triple-check my mirrors when stopping because many bikers get rear-ended when stopping for stop signs or traffic lights, so I'm always extra cautious and ready to take evasive action if necessary. So I knew that the car hadn't been there a second ago and now had suddenly appeared, solid as a rock... not a hallucination or vision of some sort.

It was a nondescript car, with nothing out of the ordinary about it. I tried to see who was inside but couldn't get a clear look.

Although it freaked me out that his car would suddenly appear out of nowhere I shrugged it off, made my turn onto the highway, and the car turned the same way that I did and was now on the highway behind me, following at a reasonable distance but close.

On this particular stretch of roadway, which was also straight and flat for miles and miles, there were no turn-offs. It was a two lane road and had no real shoulders or any place to pull over. Watching carefully in my rearview mirrors, I would have noticed if the car stopped and pulled a U-turn or pulled over.

And all of a sudden the car disappeared. The location where it was driving on the road behind me began to look somewhat hazy, a semi-solid translucent haze that I couldn't see through and then poof, the car vanished. And as soon as the car vanished, the haze cleared up completely and the view for miles and miles behind me down the straight flat highway returned.

Well...alrighty then.

Maybe my guardian angels were like, "Hey John, we're keeping an eye on you."

Thanks, guys. I appreciate it.

One other incident occurred on a lonely back road that I'm fond of riding.

I slowed to make the turn from one road to the next, and as usual I looked all around at the scenery as I decelerated. It was an open area and there wasn't anything or anyone out of the ordinary there.

I made my turn and checked my mirrors as I usually do and there behind me in the roadway was a tall, thin being, solid black in appearance. It looked to be about eight to ten feet tall, and oddly rectangular in appearance. I slowed my bike and kept watching my rearview mirrors. Sure enough, the entity was there in the flesh. I could sense that it was watching me and that it was sentient.

I thought about stopping to turn around and go back and about that time several cars, spaced fairly evenly apart, came by me from up the road, preventing me from stopping and turning around. And at about the same time I rounded a slight curve in the road and lost sight of the being anyway.

I mentally projected thoughts of goodwill toward it, and again I received the thought that there were angels, entities, beings of some sort who watched over me on the road.

As biking is a dangerous love, I'm tremendously grateful.

I had been exceptionally productive with both my painting and photography when we lived in New York, but after moving to Florida I really increased my output, especially my photographs.

I became obsessed with macro photography. Macro photography is radically close-up photography, usually of extremely small subjects and living organisms like insects, in which the size of the subject in the photograph is greater than life size.

I was astonished at the incredible detail in tiny objects such as bugs, little weed flowers, etc. I kept experimenting and I was finally able to successfully capture clear detail in a tiny weed flower that—life-size—was only the width of the head of a common straight pin.

And then the nature spirits began to get into the act, manifesting themselves in my macro photographs. Clearly discernible eyes, whole faces, the bodies of small beings, and more beings of various kinds began to show themselves in my finished work. It was astonishing and incredible, opening my eyes to an even greater understanding of the invisible realm and nature spirits.

I also loved to photograph clouds, and faces began to appear in my cloud photographs. I don't mean clouds that looked like faces; I mean faces appeared in the sky in my cloud photographs. One was so incredible that I actually jumped back from my computer when I saw it. Unbeknownst to me when I had been training my lens on the skies, the skies were looking back.

It was interesting but also a little unnerving to realize that these sky beings or cloud people are up there looking down on us all the time.

And speaking of nature spirits…one night I was sitting outside, watching the UFOs doing their thing in the sky, enjoying star gazing, when, from across the street, a glowing oblong object flew right over the peak of our neighbor's roof, headed my way.

It flew slowly enough that as it approached me I could see the details in the object, and as it flew right over me and went on by into the woods behind our home I freaked out. It was a winged fairy.

It appeared to be female. Her body was about two or three feet long. She wore clothes. She glowed as if somehow illuminated from inside, or like there was a halo of light around her entire body. She had hair, and I want to say it was blonde. And she had wings, clear wings like a dragonfly possesses. The wings were fairly large; I'd say the wingspan was probably about two feet or so.

I hollered up at her but she neither acknowledged me nor slowed the speed of her flight.

"Son of a gun," I muttered. "They are real."

Indeed, there are more things in heaven and earth than are dreamt of in our philosophies.

We had been watching shows on the paranormal that focused on haunted objects, and while perusing eBay one day I found listings for haunted dolls.

I told Marjorie about the listings and we both agreed that we should buy one.

We settled on one that had a suitably creepy description, bought her, and eagerly awaited her arrival.

We could sense a conscious being in her, but nothing paranormal ever occurred as a direct result of her presence. We welcomed her into our home and would talk to her frequently.

One night the doll came to me in a dream, thanking me for my kindness to her and for my help in releasing her. Then she disappeared in a rush of flames that swept skyward.

The next day I received an e-mail from the person from whom I bought the doll, asking if I was okay, and if our home was alright, worrying in particular if we had suffered a fire.

For she had also dreamt of the doll the same night, and saw the doll going up in flames.

The doll may not have caused any paranormal activity, but Pig Pig more than made up for that. When living in New York we were at a store that had a large display of stuffed animals, cute stuffed pigs being some of the critters displayed.

I told Marjorie, "This one's alive. He has a spirit living in him. We have to bring him home."

We named him, banally, Pig Pig.

We took Pig Pig everywhere with us, including road trips. He racked up a lot of miles in his day.

We talked to him, left the TV on for him to watch, bought him toys, and bought him little outfits to dress him up.

He responded by occasionally making quiet little noises and moving around. We would leave him in a certain position in a room, leave the room, come back later and he would have moved from the original position.

He's still good company to this day.

CHAPTER **22**

Keep a Good Sense of Humor

EVEN THOUGH MY mother had been terribly ill, and ill-tempered, not all of the family times in our old home were bad, and we did share some laughter between the three of us—my mother, my sister, and I. In the earlier years of mom's illness we even managed to hold a few dinner parties that were accompanied by much psychic phenomena.

And speaking of laughter, it has always been something of a household tradition to try and scare the wadding out of each other through various spooky practical jokes, which take on just a little more edge than might normally be anticipated when you live with so many experiences from the unseen world anyway.

Our practical jokes escalated to such an intensity that I began to lock my bedroom door at night when I went to sleep; I wasn't worried about ghosts. I was worried about my sister sneaking into my room and scaring me so damn bad she'd cause me to have a stroke.

Plus, she had reason to want revenge.

My sister lived in an apartment, which was attached to the main house, and you could also enter the apartment from inside the main house through a connecting doorway. She called me back into her apartment one night after we'd all been horsing around, joking, laughing, and having a good time, to show me some imagined anomaly she was seeing next door.

Next door stood the house where I helped care for the gentlemen who developed dementia and where I'd been saved from falling off of the stepladder by the invisible hand. The home had been converted into two apartments, and in the section of the house closest to my sister's dwelling the occupants had installed one of those bamboo window shades on one of their bedroom windows, and propped against it was one of those huge, almost life-sized Raggedy Ann dolls.

When the neighbors turned their bedroom light on, the doll would show up in sharp silhouette against the bamboo shade; at first glance it looked like a human being was sitting there. It had bugged my sister for days because the silhouette never moved, and while she was sure it must be a doll or something, she wanted my confirmation of that fact.

"It's not a person, is it John?" she asked me.

"No. It's one of those large Raggedy Ann dolls. Look, you can recognize the tell-tale signs from certain features of the silhouette."

She agreed that I was right.

"It just freaked me out," she said, "because it's been like that for days and has never moved, and it looked like a person, and I worried about some kind of foul play or something having occurred."

And I was suddenly inspired. I knew exactly how I would prank my sister that very night.

Now the story I told her and am about to relate to you is the absolute truth. It actually happened to a friend of mine with whom I worked when I once sold a certain product by appointment during evening hours.

My friend was a black man; a very dark-skinned black man. That fact is germane to the story.

This black gentleman was in the Air Force. He was stationed at our local base. With a pregnant wife to support and a new baby for which to prepare, he moonlighted with our company at night.

He was a brilliant man. A linguist, he read, wrote, and spoke several languages fluently. He was handsome. He had flair. He had a pleasant personality. He was also dignified....not reserved, or aloof, but honestly dignified. We all enjoyed his company. He had a good sense of humor, but you could tell he was a person not given to frivolity or folderol. He also appeared to be the picture of good health.

This is why we were so concerned to see him arrive in the condition he did one night: I had never seen a black man turn white, but this black man's skin was pale.

He brushed by us all with a brief "Hello" and commenced to fill out his nightly report, virtually ignoring us. We all mumbled and muttered among ourselves, wondering what the matter could be, and we finally worked up the nerve to approach him.

The first question we asked was "Are you feeling okay? Are you ill?"

"No, no. I'm fine, thanks," he replied.

His eyes never looked up from his paper, on which he was scribbling furiously.

We all exchanged glances again, and tried another tack:

"Uhm...look, we're not trying to be nosy or pry, but you're our friend, and we notice that you...well...you look awfully pale, and we were wondering—"

"It's nothing. Nothing at all," he responded.

He continued to write, never once raising his eyes to meet ours.

Again we exchanged glances and pressed on.

"Now look, not to put too fine a point on it but we've never seen a black man turn white. You're so pale it's bizarre. We know something's got to be wrong, and we'd like to know what it is. We're your friends and we'd like to help if we can."

That got a response: a kind of half-grin, and his eyes met ours for a brief moment, while he considered what to say and how to say it.

"You wouldn't believe me."

"Yes, we would. Tell us." Several of us were now invested in this conversation.

"You wouldn't believe me. You'd think I was making up a joke, or you'd make fun of me."

"No. Honestly, we wouldn't."

Well, we badgered him enough that he finally gave in and told

Keep a Good Sense of Humor

us the following story, about which the man was dead serious and in earnest.

As twilight approached he had gone to one of his few remaining appointments, and when he pulled up to the house he was somewhat taken aback. The house had large picture windows and even from the street he could see that the front room of the house was teeming with people.

His first thought was one of frustration; he had confirmed his appointment with these people, and he sat in his car for a little bit steaming about just how rude and inconsiderate they were to make an appointment with him and then host a large party instead. Unless the host and hostess were willing to tear themselves away from their guests there would be no way they would make time for him now.

His next thought was one of confusion; he looked around the street and realized that there were nowhere near enough parked cars to begin to match up with all the people he was seeing through the windows.

But his next thought clenched his course of action; he needed this sale, so he got out of his car and began walking up the long sidewalk to the home's veranda, an unusually large porch that wrapped around one side of the house. The house featured several large plate glass windows, and had several steps leading up to the spacious porch.

As he got nearer and nearer to the house, he began to experience a weird feeling that he couldn't place at first, and then he realized what it was that was giving him the willies: none of the people in the house were moving. Everyone was standing in place, perfectly still.

This, combined with the waning daylight and an interior light shining from somewhere deep within the house served to silhouette all the people standing in what appeared to be the living room of the big house. All of these factors added together began to give him an honest-to-goodness case of the creeps.

He told us that he almost turned and retreated to his car but, thinking once again of his wife and soon-to-be newborn child, he shook the weird feeling off and mounted the steps to the porch. He stopped to stare in amazement, for the figures inside were not people, but dolls—dolls of every shape and size.

Again the weird feeling returned, but he was by now determined to shake it off and continue with his sales call.

He squared his shoulders and walked to the door, and as he reached for the doorbell button, he told us: "I swear I am not making this up. Before my finger could get to the button, every single doll's head in that room turned, and they all looked at me."

He said he cleared the porch and the steps in a single bound, made it down the sidewalk to his car in a mere two or three bounding steps, then burned rubber in his haste to flee.

He was totally serious, and we could tell that he was telling us the truth.

We begged him to take us to the house so we could witness the phenomenon for ourselves, but he was adamant: no way would he ever return to that house, even if it cost him his job.

In spite of all our begging and pleading, he would not cave in.

So on this late autumn (or possibly early winter) day I told my sister this true story, cast a last glance at the doll in the window next door—knowing that she would look at the doll's silhouette and worry a little because of the spooky tale I had just shared with her—and then I planned my next course of action as I left her apartment and went back into the main house.

I waited until I knew she would be settled in to watch television, sitting on a couch across the room from a window that I knew she would leave open while she watched TV. Even though it was late autumn or early winter it was a warm night, and I knew she would have the window open for ventilation. Right below that window was another couch, upon the back of which her two small dogs would lie, keeping a sharp lookout for the neighborhood cat that came to taunt and tease them. (The cat was an orange-colored tabby and was the only cat I had seen in the neighborhood since moving home other than Gizmo's ghost.)

I snuck quietly out the back door of the house, hunching down to creep by her living room windows at a level where I knew she couldn't see me if she were to look, and I got so tickled at the prospect of what I was going to do that I had to stifle my laughter.

Adding to my difficulty in staying quiet were the crisp fallen leaves scattered in abundance on the ground, and I was wondering how I'd make it through them and get to her open window without their crunching giving me away.

The little dogs were no problem...I knew that they'd work in my favor to lure her to the window eventually.

So, trying to avoid the crunchy leaves in the dark, stifling my snickering to the best of my ability, I finally made it underneath her open window. By then her little dogs were both on their short, stubby legs, barking for all they were worth.

I could peek under their little bellies as they stood on the back of the couch and see my sister sitting on the couch across the room, watching the TV and yelling at them to hush their barking.

Every time they'd quieten down a little I'd poke at the window screen and get them started all over again.

"Oh for pity sakes hush," my sister thundered, "it's just the old cat."

I kept poking at them, and they kept barking, and finally I achieved my objective: my sister arose from the couch and walked across the room to peer out into the darkness, trying to see what the dogs were raising all the ruckus about.

As soon as she stuck her face against the window screen, I popped up, jamming my face against the screen right into hers, my eyes bulging as wide as I could make them.

"Oh my god," my sister yelled, and she jumped back so far I thought she was going to fall over. Her eyes were wide with fright, and her mouth hung open as she defensively clutched at her chest.

And then it hit her.

I began to run for the back door to the house with all my speed, laughing out loud as I went, trying to get inside before my sister recovered her senses, but I couldn't make it.

Her door burst open.

"John, you crazy son-of-a-bitch. What the hell are you trying to do, scare the life out of me? Where are you?"

By this time, our neighbors' lights were coming on, and a few other doors were opening as well.

Mom heard the ruckus and wondered what in the world was going on, and of course my sister chased me back into the house. I laughed so hard I nearly fell over, and we all had a round of laughter as my sister told our mom what I had done to her.

That's one of the reasons Sis wanted revenge, and the chief reason I kept my bedroom door locked when I went to bed at night. It had nothing to do with ghosts.

One night as I lay on my back, sound asleep, I awoke with a hand grasping my entire face.

Thinking I was struggling with the remnants of some nightmarish dream, I instead rapidly realized that there was indeed a large hand grasping my face.

I grabbed the hand at its wrist, which was solid and real. I knew the hand wasn't mine because I felt no sensation in my left arm when I grabbed it. I forcefully threw the hand off me with my right hand, sprang out of bed ready to fight, and laughed so loudly I was afraid I'd wake up the entire house when I faced an empty room and my completely numb left arm swinging in slowing arcs as it dangled by my side with absolutely no feeling whatsoever.

I feel sure that those on the Other Side must get just as tickled at these incidents as we do.

When Marjorie and I still lived in upstate New York I had a good buddy there, Bill Yeoman, who introduced me to Black Rock Forest, an astonishingly beautiful place that we both loved to photograph.

We would tromp all over the forest, so naturally we both wore somewhat old and raggedy clothes that we wouldn't mind getting dirty or torn. And we both had beards; that fact will become relevant in a moment.

Every now and then busses brought groups of kids from New York City, or elsewhere, to the forest for a field trip, but most of the time the forest was quiet wherever we roamed in it, and many times we wouldn't even see another person.

We had gone downhill and to the right, over to one of the lakes, and were happily engaged in making photos when all of a sudden the forest erupted with noise. Kids—lots of kids—yelling, screaming, and laughing. We rolled our eyes at each other and continued to take our photographs.

We both used tripods in order to get the sharpest images possible, and rather than collapse them we would leave them at shooting height, fold the legs together, and hoist them up over our shoulders with our cameras still securely attached and at the ready, much as you'd shoulder a rifle.

Our path took us back around the bend and uphill where there was a large yellow school bus parked and a bunch of teenage kids milling around, still making noise. As we began to top the rise little by little the kids began to go silent, some pointing at us, all of them staring wide-eyed, some with mouths gaping.

As we got closer to the bus it suddenly grew so quiet that you could have heard the proverbial pin drop in that forest.

Bill and I looked at each other, shrugged, and continued up the rise and now saw a woman trying to walk toward us, literally bent over double with laughter.

This caused Bill and me to look at each other again, like, "What in the world are we walking into?"

When the woman got close to us and finally caught her breath, she explained that she was the kids' teacher, and that before we had rounded the curve and started uphill she had been regaling them with a legendary tale about two old crazy hermit brothers living deep within the forest, who were bearded, wore scruffy, dirty clothes, were reputed to be a little crazy, and who carried their guns around with them to hunt game and possibly punish trespassers, etc.

About that time, we started up the hill: bearded, wearing scruffy, dirty clothes, and probably looking a little crazy, with our tripods resting on our shoulders, which—from a distance—could easily be mistaken for rifles or shotguns.

We shared a laugh with the teacher and walked on our way, past the kids, who continued to watch our every movement, eyes wide, still silent. If you could only have seen their shocked faces. One of the best experiences ever, and we still share a laugh over it to this day.

CHAPTER **23**

Farewell for Now

WELL, IT'S ABOUT time to say goodbye to this set of adventures. I'll leave you with one last experience that made a dynamic impression on me and the intensity of it has stayed with me ever since it happened.

I hope that it will impress upon you the magnitude of the invisible realm with which we deal, and that it might inspire you to seek your own intimacy with the Other Side, invoking its help, protection, and guidance.

It had been raining, and there were some occasional rumbles of thunder. The rain now stopped, and the thunder quieted. It was still overcast, and I stepped outside to look up at the sky and watch the clouds flying swiftly by.

I had been thinking about what a blessed and charmed life I've led, and how happy I was in my current circumstances here at our Florida home.

With genuine gratitude I continued to gaze at the sky, raised my arms up and said aloud, "Thank you."

A voice rumbled from within the sudden sound of thunder, the words clear and distinct.

"You're welcome," it said.

The End

I hope that reading this book and the true stories it contains has challenged you, made you cry, made you laugh, given you food for thought, helped and inspired you, and yes…even entertained you.

I appreciate you taking the time to buy and read my book. Thank you.

From whichever bookseller you purchased your copy, if you could please return there and leave me a five-star rating, it would mean the world to me. Yes, I do check my ratings and my reviews.

A five-star review is not a luxury or a nod to the ego of an author; your five-star review helps my book become more visible to other shoppers in a site's rankings; it expresses to other shoppers that, in your opinion, my book is a good read and worth their time and money; it also lets me know that I'm on the right track with my writing and that you've enjoyed my book.

If you haven't already, please also consider buying a copy of my previous book, *Riding with Ghosts, Angels, and the Spirits of the Dead*. More information can be found about that book at: http://www.ridingwithghosts.net

If you'd like to purchase a psychic reading with me I welcome new clients. Complete information about my psychic services can be found at: http://www.johnrussell.net

May God bless you, prosper you, heal you, strengthen you, and shine light on you.

—John Russell

Lightning Source UK Ltd.
Milton Keynes UK
UKHW020809190122
397392UK00009B/360

9 781977 239372